Tails of Unconditional Love

Your Journey to the Other Side of Pet Loss Grief

PAM BAREN KAPLAN

TAILS OF UNCONDITIONAL LOVE

Your Journey to the Other Side of Pet Loss Grief

By Pam Baren Kaplan

Paws to Celebrate Publishing
2137 Silver Linden Lane
Buffalo Grove, Illinois 60089
www.pawstocelebrate.life

ISBN-13: 978-0-578-53703-0

Illustrations by Kris D. Carr
Editing by Dana Micheli
Cover by Transcendent Publishing
Interior Formatting/Design by Shanda Trofe
Author Photography by Rick Reeves and Jerry Attere

Printed in the United States of America.

To Roxanne “Roxy” Ophelia Kaplan, who came into my life in my mid-forties and showed me it was never too late for a great childhood. My unwavering, eternal unconditional love for her is the reason for this book.

Acknowledgements

To My Girls

Zuzu and Frankie, my 4-legger loves that I am so grateful for. You have tolerated so many days with Mama's face to the computer making this book happen. And to my other love, 4-legger grandoggie, Penny.

And To My 2-Leggers

My husband Lou for blessing this project, *I love yous*.

To my kids; Jon, Dani and Adrianne.

To my Pack Test Group: Brenda Giles, Jan Dicker, Jay Canfield, Liza Linder, Paula Almilli Ayala, Terry Traynor and Theresa Schreiber.

And to my entire Pack at Paws to Celebrate, you have inspired me. I couldn't do this without you! A special thanks to my Pack within a Pack: my admins, Cindy Collard, Jay Canfield, Jan Dicker and Edwena Martin!

And to all the angels watching over us from the *Paws Pack Subdivision* at *The Bridge*, thank you so much. Until we meet again!

And to a very special angel who helped make this book come to life. I celebrate and honor you, Ran.

I love you all to the BIG moon and back, 11 times infinity!

Your Road Map

Many times I've been asked,
"How will I know that I'm
healed?"

I respond, "When that tear of
liquid love gently meets your
smile, then you know you are
getting close."

-Pam Baren Kaplan

Section One

Where the Journey Begins

Introduction

Welcome! I congratulate you for being here. This is a "ruff" step in the right direction for healing your grief over the loss of your pet.

How do I know? Because I've been where you are right now. With no professional guidance or resources to get me through the dark days, I had to learn a lot through trial and error, and of course, with the help of my guardian angel. I'd like to tell you a little about her and my journey.

I grew up in a single-parent home. We lived in a small apartment in Chicago—me, my younger sister Lisa and our mom. We weren't poor, but we weren't rich either, which meant certain things weren't in the budget for me… certain things like a dog. Many of my friends had a pet, and oh how I envied them! When hanging out at their homes after school I often spent more time playing with their furry friends than I did with them. I longed for my own furry someone to love and to love me right back, but all my begging and pleading fell on deaf ears. Now don't get me wrong, Mom *tried.* She gave in and got me a turtle and a few lame goldfish, but I never had my own dog. It seemed there was always a reason (or as I called them, *excuses*) why.

"We live in an apartment," Mom would say, "This is no place for a dog and the landlord wouldn't allow it!"

The cat situation was more clear-cut. "Out of the question," she'd say, "and don't bring it up again. You know I'm deathly allergic."

I went pet-less for my entire childhood and much of my adulthood.

Finally, when I was thirty-seven, my dream came true in the form of a chubby yellow Lab. We named her Roxy (short for Roxanne) and she took up residence in my heart as if she had always lived there. She was my everything, my baby, my best friend, and my protector. She was family.

From the start, Roxy was a true character and made everything an event. After she "did her business," she would wipe all four paws on the grass and elegantly trot into the house like she was in a pageant. Mostly, though, she just loved to be loved. As long as you were touching her, she was happy. She was a great sibling to her 2-legged brother Jon and sister Dani. Roxy was always a ready and willing plaything. My daughter never played with a doll in her life. Why would she even entertain the idea, when there was this huge, overly enthusiastic stuffed animal that never minded having socks tied on her ears as pigtails or being dressed up in an old Far Side sweatshirt to play Keep-Away in the yard?

Roxy loved everything and everyone except being wet or in water! I ask you, *What kind of Lab doesn't like water*? No matter that she had her own twenty-four-foot above ground deluxe swimming pool in our backyard. She wanted nothing to do with it.

When I was forty-four years old, I was diagnosed with Type 2 diabetes. My doctor read me the riot act, the central message being: "Get some exercise! Get your butt outside and walk!"

I looked at my yella girl and said, "Okay, if I have to do it, you're going with me!"

Roxy had no complaints.

We began walking each morning and at dusk, and eventually got so into it we'd be gone for an hour each time. We even walked when we were on vacation. It was so peaceful, and a great bonding experience for us.

Our favorite walk time was sunset. She'd always walk slightly ahead of me, and every now and then she'd turn back and look at me with those huge dark brown eyes just to see if I was okay. I loved watching her shadow bounce against the sidewalk illuminated by the streetlights. I'd think to myself how lucky I was, to have the best yella dog in the world. What a wonderful life!

As the years passed, my girl began showing signs of aging. Some arthritis in the hip, sleeping more than she did and an occasional *poop ball* left in her bed. My heart was beginning to feel the future. But as long as she had that ravenous Lab-a-tite and greeted me every night when I came home from work, I told myself, "We're okay, we're still doing okay."

Of course, her decline was inevitable. Unable to walk well without the support of a wall, losing her sight and hearing, she had become an incontinent old girl deserving more love and attention than ever before. I had no complaints. I willingly obliged.

On the morning of January 31, 2011, Roxy and my husband had a little one-on-one. Later he told me that she had looked into his eyes and said, *Pop,* (yes, that's what she called him), *it's time. I have held this family together for nearly seventeen years and I am worn out. You gotta help me."*

With tears in his voice he called me to come home from work.

"It's time," he said.

The drive home from downtown Chicago to the northern burbs of Illinois was surreal. I just remember being sick to my stomach knowing what was ahead of me.

Both kids, now adults, came home to see their sister off. My daughter gently wrapped Roxy in her favorite old blanket and held her close like she had done so many times since childhood. She then carried her precious sister to the car for one last ride.

Arriving at the animal hospital, we were escorted to a private family room. The vet came in and explained step by step what would happen. He excused himself to give us a few moments alone with her.

We surrounded her, holding her close, telling her how much she meant to each one of us, that she was the best puppy ever. I spoke softly in her ear and told her how much she would be missed, but most importantly, that she'd better haunt us every day!

"I'm counting on you," I cried in whispers.

The vet returned and asked if we were ready. *Ready?* I would never be ready to let this love of my life go. My heart was already shattering into a million pieces. We cried. I held her in my arms, I buried my tear-soaked face into hers. I felt her last breath, and she peacefully went to sleep.

Roxy lived almost seventeen years, a good long time for a Lab, but for me, *forever, would never be long enough. What I wouldn't have given to try!*

I then faced another decision I had never had to make before: what to do with "her." Collectively, my family decided to have her individually cremated so we could keep her ashes with us. A good thing we did, because they would come in handy over this journey.

As we walked into our house - empty and silent for the first time in nearly two decades – we realized that Roxy's passing had changed our family forever. We also realized something else – that precious girl had indeed been the glue holding us together.

Each of us dealt with our sadness differently. My husband and I didn't speak much to each other, let alone in full sentences. I so desperately missed Roxy and found myself angrily second-guessing so many things. *Why I hadn't given her one more hug when I had the chance? Did she know how much I loved her? Did I love Roxy enough? Did I spend enough time with her? And the biggie: "Did I do the right thing? Could she have lived a few more days? Could we have held on for more time together?* I felt so insecure and hopeless, guilty and grief-stricken. Such is the nature of being a 2-legger.

Soon my overwhelming sadness turned into full-blown depression. I stopped walking, stopped taking care of myself. I became a human sloth living in that dark place for what seemed like an eternity. Everything suffered - my family and friendships, as well as my job. People at work didn't understand what was going on with me. I was disconnected.

One day, I was off in some far-away land, daydreaming about Rox when suddenly I heard my boss' voice:

"Hey, Pam…come back to Earth… it was just a f*%king dog! Get over it! Just go buy another one!"

The entire office was witness to this, and I was mortified. My face flushed hot and tears began to flood my eyes.

Has someone ever said something that you knew had changed you forever? Do you remember the day, the moment it happened? Well, this was the moment of truth for me. Would I worry over losing a paycheck or should I give him a piece of my mind?

"F*&k you right back!" I shouted, then walked out of my office crying.

My boss didn't fire me, but he never apologized either. After that day, I learned not to assume that people who have or had a pet will have the same level feeling I did for Roxy. I came to understand that to some people, a pet is an accessory one owns, a part of an image someone wants to portray. My boss was in that category. I *almost* felt sorry for him because he obviously hadn't experienced the bond, the depth of the purest love of all - unconditional love.

I also realized I could not go on sleepwalking through my life. After much soul-searching, I declared, "Human sloth, no more!" It was time to start walking again. That wasn't going to be easy. Stubborn, resistant and plain old scared, I dreaded going without my trusty yella partner next to me. I desperately needed to feel my angel was always with me, periodically looking back making sure I was okay. I needed a little spiritual push!

A co-worker suggested I wear a "cremains necklace," a piece of jewelry that contained Roxy's ashes. At first I was a bit weirded out, but the longer I thought about it I found the idea gave me some comfort. It was time to go shopping.

I looked at so many pet memorials but never found anything that felt right. They were too mass-produced, not me at all. Finally I decided, I'm going to make it myself! That way I could combine two of my loves: Roxy and crafting jewelry.

At that time I had a little side business, "The Bored Executive's Jewelry," working with wire, gemstones and crystals to create Tree of Life pendants. The Tree of Life is a powerful spiritual symbol represented in almost every belief system; my pendants were what I affectionately called "bohemian hippie-style" pieces. My business name was not completely tongue-in-cheek either. While I wasn't exactly bored at work, I did need stress relief from my sixty-plus-hour-week, not including a three-hour roundtrip commute.

One afternoon while working on a tree, the idea came to me: what if I could incorporate Roxy's ashes into a polymer as a bead, and the bead would be the leaves of the tree? A little firing, drilling, polishing and wiring later, and I had created "Roxy's Tree" and the first of many Trees of Unconditional Love and Life. It would also be the first – and very profound – step in my healing.

When I put the piece on for the first time, I felt a shiver, a warm tingle in my body. I felt Roxy with me, not only *in* my heart, but worn close to my heart.

I smiled and said, "I am never going anywhere without you girl."

I know in my heart and soul that she agreed.

I received many compliments on Roxy's Tree. I found it amusing to see people's reactions when I'd tell them that the beautiful piece contains my dog's ashes. Some were compassionate animal lovers and ask for my card, while others ran the other way. But at the end of the day, what others thought was immaterial – my little side business (or as my tax accountant called it, "your hobby") was helping to heal the hole in my heart. I began to wonder if I could make other necklaces, help other people who had lost their pet as well.

Life often feels like a barrage of incidents flying at us faster than we can handle them. If you're like me, you believe these incidents are really lessons we need to learn. That doesn't mean, however, that I don't occasionally look up at the heavens, shake my fist and ask, "Excuse me, but can we slow down the pace just a smidge?" The lesson I was about to have thrown at me was life-changing; I didn't like it one bit, but looking back, it was necessary for my personal and spiritual growth. I'll give you the condensed version of the drama. Hang on - it is time for a slight plot twist!

Looking back, 2011 was not one of my stellar years. Less than 10 months after Roxy's passing, I was about to grieve once more. After thirty-two years making a cushy six-figure salary as Senior Account Executive and Director of Human Resources and Operations of a Chicago-based market research company, I lost my job.

"Position eliminated," I was bluntly told.

I thought my life was over. I cried. I put the covers over my head to shut everyone out. I ate a few gallons of fat free ice cream to drown my sorrows. I drank, and I drank some more. I didn't shower. I was a real piece of work to live with. I was becoming the sequel, "The Sloth, Part Two."

Even in my distress, I reminded myself to be grateful for the full year of severance. At least I was able to help keep a roof over my head, feed the family and have some time to plan my next move. I had always loved the "people" part of my corporate job. I thrived on watching employees find happiness and balance in their personal and professional life. So, after much consideration, I decided to go back to school to become a certified corporate and life coach. The more I thought about it, I felt it was my calling.

After becoming certified I took a position giving seminars in professional adult education, both publicly and for private organizations. There were as many as a hundred attendees at these classes, and over the next four years, I met wonderful people from many backgrounds and walks of life; I also learned a great deal about who I am and what I am capable of doing. The real payoff came at the end of my seminars when students would crowd around me, thanking me for sharing what I knew to help them do their job. I felt respected; I felt confident. I felt better than I had in a long time.

I was also exhausted. My schedule required me to be in an airport at least twice a week and spend countless hours in a car, driving hundreds of miles from one seminar to another. I was getting sick from breathing recycled air and shaking hands with hundreds of people a week. And yet I kept pushing myself, until a nasty bout of pneumonia forced me to take a break. I was mentally and physically worn down.

When I get sick I am not a model patient. I get crabby because I feel like I'm not being productive. When my husband can't take it anymore, he throws me the remote control and says, "Go rest," then disappears, leaving me alone to overthink for hours. Needless to say, I drove myself nuts.

One day, my brave daughter sat down on my germ-infested bed, looked deep into my angst-ridden eyes, and asked "What's going on?"

"I'm not satisfied with what I'm doing," I whined, sounding very much like an eight-year-old about to throw a tantrum, "I want to do more, I want to make a difference."

I then told her about the people in my seminars who had come up to me at the end of class and complimented Roxy's Tree. This would open the emotional floodgates, as they poured out their own stories of love and loss. Each time it touched my soul to see these people come alive as they talked about their memories. One woman thanked me for validating her grief, justifying her right to mourn a pet! I found this need for validation a common thread among my students who stayed "after class" to have pet-talk with the teacher, and I longed to help these people, and others, on a deeper level. But how to reach them? Certainly there had to be a better venue for healing than in a post-seminar lecture hall.

"Why not try starting a Facebook group for people who have lost their pets," Dani suggested?

That conversation was the beginning of Paws to Celebrate, which I launched on August 14 of 2015. Upon hearing the name, a few friends looked at me sideways and said it was a bit too cheesy, but when you feel something in your heart and your gut agrees, it's a marriage made in heaven, or in this case at the Rainbow Bridge. Paws to Celebrate reflected my belief and mission that the lives of all family members – including the furry, finned and feathered ones – were meant to be celebrated.

Initially, membership consisted of a few friends and family who were pet parents. I began searching Facebook for people who had lost their pets, then I would send my condolences and invite them to the group. Between my efforts and word of mouth, new members started pouring in. Today, we are over 5,000 members strong and growing. We have become a "Pack," and I am affectionately known as "*The Leader of The Pack.*"

A few months passed, and though I was thrilled about the growth of the group, I still felt that something was missing. That gut of mine was nagging at me again, telling me that I needed knowledge and credibility in grief work. That's when I went back for additional training and became a certified grief recovery specialist with a focus on pet loss grief recovery. I was feeling that confidence again. Life was feeling pretty good.

It was February of 2016, and I was scheduled to teach a five-day run in Alaska. Alaska in February? Yay – dark by three p.m.! And to top it off, I was teaching in a different town each day. This meant travelling in a tiny little plane each night. Yay times five! The trip went reasonably well, though the best part was getting bumped to first class on the way back to Chicago. Now, that was something to celebrate. I landed in O'Hare with a smile on my face and anticipating some much-deserved R&R.

Instead, a few days after returning home, my old pal pneumonia decided to pay a visit. I was given a round of strong antibiotics, an inhaler and orders to remain in bed. Not exactly the R&R I had been expecting. I was grounded.

After a week, I hadn't improved. I called my doctor, who recommended a trip to the ER.

"Let them do a chest X-ray, maybe a nebulizer treatment, and hopefully that helps."

The thought of going to the ER at ten p.m. in my jammies, especially in March, wasn't one bit entertaining; in fact, I might have blown it off if it weren't for my daughter herding me into her car.

"You're going to the ER, no argument!" she commanded. She'd always been a very bossy kid, just like her mom.

What happened next was a shock. After a few tests, the emergency room doctor told us, "Your pneumonia is gone, but your heart is dying."

What? This can't be!

I thought that this would all blow over and I'd go home that afternoon, but when we received the results of the angiogram it got real, very real: All four major arteries were blocked. Then the doctor delivered another surprise: I was not a candidate for a coronary stent, but I was at the head of the class for a quadruple bypass.

As my family freaked out around me, I found myself to be oddly calm. I wasn't afraid of the surgery, or in the worst-case scenario - dying. I knew "someone" was in my corner. I felt confident that my guardian angel was watching over me. I believed Roxy was right there every step of the way, making sure I was okay.

I came through what turned out to be *only* a triple bypass -still serious, but all went well. I had been given another chance at life, and I was determined to make it count. I knew Roxy had a paw in my next moves, and I had to make her proud of her mama. I decided to dedicate my career solely to pet loss grief recovery.

Bringing this book to life is in celebration and honor of Roxy. Just as she was my beloved friend and exercise partner during her life, she is now my muse, guiding me to help bring comfort and healing to all who struggle with pet loss.

As you embark upon this journey, I will share much more about understanding and getting to know your grief; nurturing the pain, and, finally, transforming it into love. In this book you will find your voice and a space to tell your personal, unconditional love story, or "tail," as I like to call it. I will bring you into The Pack and share a few tails myself. And know this, you're never alone; I'll be here the entire time, walking just slightly ahead of you and looking back periodically to be sure *you* are doing okay.

Terminology

The following is a list of words, phrases, quotes or acronyms used in this book. I thought that this might be a good idea so that you, my dear reader, are comfortable with my Pamism *PawSpeak*.

A.R.F. – Always Remembered Forever

Note: My son Jon and daughter-in-law Adrianne claim that I "stole" the word arf!; I say, that while this may be true, I am the one who *decoded* the acronym.

ASAPawsable – As Soon as Pawsable (Okay, *possible.)*

AWA – Angel Wing Announcement: The weekly Sunday celebration of the Paws to Celebrate Pack of the angels who have earned their wings.

Badge of Unconditional Love – A spiritual badge worn by pet parents who have dedicated their lives to unconditionally giving and receiving eternal love from their pet. It is "fur-ever."

de-Tails – Providing the entire story, right down to the very last detail!

Worst Firsts – The first twelve months of triggers following the passing of your pet.

Liquid Love – Very special tears cried by pet parents

Pack – n. Our community of pet parents

Pack – v. To accept one into the Paws community – "The Pack"

Telepathic Text – Spontaneous thoughts about your loved one who has passed

Unpack – v. To remove from The Pack for un-pack-like behavior

P.E.T. – Positive Energy Therapist

P.L.G. – Pet Loss Grief

RUFF – Really Un-Fair Feelings; also: rough or difficult

Tails – Tales, or stories

2-Legger – A person of the human being variety

4-Legger – A companion with feathers, fins, scales, tails, hooves or any other animal of the non-2-legger variety

What You Will Gain From "Participating" In This Book

This book is more than just a collection of stories, told in (what I hope) in my humorous tone. It is a tool of hope, designed to elicit what I call the "three "Cs" - courage, confidence and compassion. That said, I will share some of my personal journey, a smattering of experiences from my clients and cite a few research studies, books and articles to help you get through to the "other side" of pet loss grief.

What will you learn from reading this book?

- You have every right to grieve your pet as a family member.
- You are not alone on this journey.
- You are normal.
- How to find your authentic voice, raw as it may be at times, to tell your love story, in your own words exactly as you intend, even if it means rehashing it over and over again until you feel it's perfect.
- You are spiritually liberated to believe as you want.
- You *can* see this journey through, and so much more!

Who Is This Book Written For?

Good chance that you were drawn to this book because you have experienced a great loss, or perhaps you are preparing for one. You may be grieving a loss from minutes, months or years ago. Everyone grieves in their own way. This book will help those in the early days, as well as those whose hearts are still breaking a decade after the loss.

At the writing of this book, my Roxy has been an angel for eight years. Though I still grieve her, I've accepted and forged a new normal in which she's by my side in spirit rather than trotting in front of me as we take our evening walk. It took a lot of time and inner work for me to get to this place, and I know that many people struggle in silence for years. They don't complete the grieving process but instead try to bury it and get on with life. But that's the thing about grief, if you don't work through it, it becomes like a growth that's always there, paining and hindering you. This book is for everyone who wants to remove that growth and move forward with their life.

Finally, this book is intended for those who are trying to change or improve on the way they were taught about grief as a child.

When I was a child, most parents tried to shield their kids from the death of their pet. They would fret about what to say to their young son or daughter, then, instead of presenting the truth in an honest, age-appropriate way, they would end up telling him/her a white lie about where the pet went. When he or she is a little older, and able to handle it, they'll reveal the truth. In the meantime, the child goes around thinking that "Ranger" went to live on a farm up in Wisconsin with horses and apple trees. When and if the parents do share the truth, when the child learns that they were lied to, mistrust is born. Not good. Today, parents tend to take the view that (age-appropriate) honesty is the best policy. More about healing the heart of a child later on.

For the Times They Are A-Changing... Slowly

Grieving the loss of a pet has changed, not only for children, but adults as well. Until fairly recently losing a pet was something you didn't *publicly* make a big deal out of for fear of judgement or ridicule.

Over the past ten to fifteen years, however, it has become more socially acceptable for pet parents to memorialize their animal companion. They are requesting the same types of services only once offered to 2-leggers. Pet loss is becoming big business to the funeral industry. One funeral home director reported that back in 2003 he was doing only nine individual cremations a week, whereas today the number exceeds two hundred!

Pet loss grief is being recognized by therapists and behavior specialists as something that *we should not ignore* but pay close attention to.

Corporations have also been changing their way of thinking. Take a look at how many leading-edge firms have a "Bring Your Dog to Work Day." Some companies even allow dogs to come every day! Why? Animals encourage a positive social environment, help break the ice, creates smoother pathways to teamwork and a general sense of happiness in the workplace.

During my many years in HR I've witnessed changes in the wording of bereavement policies. Yet even I was shocked when I read that pets were to be included in such policies as family members! Slowly but surely, we are getting there, thanks in part to the research on the benefits of companion animals, and that the bond between animals and humans is more freely discussed both at home and in the workplace.

Participate in This Book?

In a word, yes. Reading about this journey will get you only about 50% of the way; in order to truly facilitate healing, you need to take the actions steps. And the same goes for those of you jumping right into the journaling sections without reading the rest. In order to get where you want to be, you need to know how all the pieces of the process fit together, and where you fit into it.

Think of it this way: if you were a carpenter, would you show up to work without all the necessary tools to get the job done, and done well? Of course not. The same is true here. The information and education preceding the journaling is like your toolkit; you want to be very clear on why and how to use these tools to get the work done efficiently. The journaling itself is when you strike the hammer to the nail. Remember this if you are tempted to use shortcuts.

Also remember that I'm here, walking this path with you to help you achieve your goals.

Goals as a Benchmark

Right now you may be thinking, *Hang on a second! Who said anything about goals? I just want to feel better.*

The thing is, feeling better *is* a goal; you simply have to define what feeling better *means for you.* Before beginning this journey, take some time to ask yourself, "Where do I *want* to be?" I know you may not have a specific answer at the top of your mind but answering a few questions below might help you figure it out.

Setting Initial Goals

What did (Pet's Name) ______________________ mean to you?

____

____

____

What did you gain from your relationship with __________ over the years?

____

____

____

When _______________ passed, describe what you went through emotionally, physically and spiritually?

____

____

____

Remember, you can always come back and modify what you wrote today, so don't put pressure on yourself to get it "right." That is why this is called a journey, not a quick grief fix. But for now, ask yourself how you see yourself getting to the other side of grief? What are your goals? What do you hope to gain from participating and interacting with this book? Please take a moment and write down the first thing that comes to you. What else do you hope to gain from this book?

____

____

____

Good job! Now I need to explain…

What You Won't Get from This Book

I need to be upfront, totally transparent and yes, very clear. There are two things I cannot do. It doesn't matter how much you "pretty please" me, beg, grovel or attempt to bribe me. You can even scream and throw a tantrum – it won't work.

First, I can't bring your love back to you in the physical form that you knew. We will discuss spirituality later in the book, but for now suffice it to say I don't have that power!

Second, I can't take the pain of your grief away like magic. Nope.

"*What?!*" you may be saying, "If you can't take my pain away why am I reading and participating in this book?"

Hang on a second and I'll explain. Simply put, you've earned this pain! Yes, that's what I said, you *earned* it, and believe it or not you wouldn't want me to take it away even if I could. To do this, I'd have to erase your memory of these fantastic life experiences you cherish! I'd have to change time and the memories would all be obliterated! Again, this is a skillset I simply do not possess.

Here's a little example that I like to share with my clients. Taking away the struggles and pain of life would look a lot like George Bailey's angelic intervention from the Frank Capra holiday classic, *It's A Wonderful Life.* If you haven't seen it, George Bailey, played by Jimmy Stewart, is an all-around nice guy who sacrifices his dreams to help others and one Christmas Eve finds himself in a lot of hot water. He's contemplating ending it all when Clarence, an angel-in-training, steps in to help. He listens as George rants about his litany of problems, then states that he wishes he'd never been born at all. Wish granted! George is given an amazing gift that night

– he is able to see all the ways he positively affected the world, and what things would be like it he had never been around. At the end (and I'm sorry to give it away if you haven't seen it), George is grateful for everything he has, including the painful and disappointing times. Above all, it's a movie about gratitude.

Now stop for a second and think, what would your life look like if your pet had never been born, never entered your life? What would you have missed? A lot, I'm sure.

Gratitude for our own wonderful lives is where we need to be. This means accepting that you've "earned" your special pain. I call this, wearing The Badge of Unconditional Love. Once bitten by unconditional love, it's *fur-ever.* This is a big step toward healing.

Your Path to Healing

Here's what this book and I can offer: the tools to get you on the path to healing, and in a safe space to do it. This is a space free from judgment and ridicule. A space where there is no being compared to weird Aunt Jane crying over the loss of one of her eight cats, or oddball Uncle Richard who is always talking to his dog Rusty, though no one has seen the animal since Thanksgiving 2017.

On the other hand, this journey also brings you into The Pack, an amazing global community of 2-leggers who have come together after the passing of their beloved family member. Here, you have an opportunity to be who you are and in the company of other likeminded people who truly understand what you've been through. You will find acceptance, hope, and the time you need to grieve for as long as you need, not what someone else deems appropriate. I will share more about The Pack and becoming "packed" at the conclusion of this book.

At points throughout this book, I will include some Pamism "Pawspeak" and wisdom from The Pack. There will be quotes from some very special 2-leggers who are senior members of The Pack, who helped develop what you are experiencing today, because they also went through it. They have allowed me to share the insights, emotions and celebrations they experienced along the way. I am very grateful to each and every one of them who used this journal as a tool for their healing. Right now you may be wondering, *How did journaling help them heal? How can it help me?*

I was hoping you'd ask!

Journaling… What are the Benefits?

Long before the Internet, long before online 24/7 therapists advertised by gold medal athletes, there was journaling.

Journaling was my saving grace, during the dark ages – also known as my pre-teen years – when I was an awkward, overweight, taller-than-most-of-the-boys ugly duckling. I felt lost and unloved, like I was perpetually the new kid on the block. I needed an outlet for my pubescent drama, which, I was convinced, no one would ever understand. No one that is except for my diary, or journal.

My diary was my best friend. I could tell it whatever I needed to without censoring myself one word! I could embellish, add a little more drama if I chose to do so. Why not? I was writing for me, and me alone (except for the time when my kids found my diary and read every embarrassing de-Tail, but that's a story for another time!) The point is, unless you decide to share it, your journal is an extension of your private world, a place that's safe for yourself.

Safe and Judgement Free

Journaling is a means of self-expression. Whenever you start writing on that blank sheet of paper or you type away at the keyboard, you can be whomever you want to be, regurgitating your emotions without fear of judgment.

Journaling allows our brain to slow down and deal with these emotions. These feelings may very well trigger tears as you tell your tail; painful as this may be, it is also a crucial part of healing and grief recovery. Tear talk to be covered in a little bit…

Healing Can Be Measurable

Grief journaling can improve self-insight. Going back after a week or two and rereading an entry lets you know how you were dealing with your raw emotions at that time and illuminate the changes you've made since then. This is a benchmark to help you measure your healing. Even the smallest improvements are to be celebrated.

In Your Own Voice

Journaling allows you to tell your tail that – let's face it - no one else really wants to hear. No matter how loving your family and friends are, eventually they will tire of hearing the same diatribe about the passing of your pet. It could be a week or a month, but at some point they will decide it's time for you to move on, even if you're not ready to.

Your journal will not push back; it will patiently listen as you write with your heart. Writing is a way of giving voice to the story that you have been aching to tell. Your journal has the open-mindedness to hear your story even if it means rehashing it over and over and over again until you are ready to move past it and toward the next step in your healing.

Your Most Trusted Confidant

Your journal is your most trusted friend during the solitary process of grief. Grieving can be very lonely. You may feel like an outsider or, as I referred to it earlier, that "perpetual new kid on the block." This is not the time to bury emotions but share them with someone or "something" you trust.

No Thick Skin Required

Until one has experienced grief, they can't completely understand the complicated array of emotions.

We live in a culture that is still averse to 2-legger grief rituals with regard to people, let alone pets! I've seen and heard people struggle for the appropriate words of condolences, only to spew sentiments that actually diminish the grief of the person they are trying to comfort.

In your journal, you will find the safety to write in the raw voice of pain. This will help you begin to forge the new normal narrative of your history.

Fear of Forgottens

Life is rapidly happening around us and so easy for things to get placed in storage somewhere in the back of our mind. We're 2-leggers, we forget. Journaling is an effective way to dust off and shake loose those memories.

Before starting their journal, a few of my clients told me they were afraid they wouldn't have enough to tell, or that they had forgotten so many of the stories from years past. This is a common fear. These same clients later told me that the exercises in this book actually helped stimulate their memories. Many even found that they were smiling as they relived precious moments with their pet. As one client shared, "I'm feelin' the healin'!"

Memories may not appear at the very moment you try and conjure them all up, so don't stress. These little vignettes seem to infiltrate your thoughts when you don't expect them. It may surprise you that a moment of clarity comes to you while brushing your teeth, or snarfing down a quick breakfast. I recommend the voice recording app on your phone or a little note pad for these spontaneous recollections. These are telepathic texts, to be recorded or written down as they are "gifted" to you. More on this later.

Redemption

Journaling can help you find redemption after a loss. As we will discuss in more de-Tail later in this book, guilt can be a heavy-handed emotion in grieving. Taking on the blame for your pet's passing is unfair to yourself, especially because at the time you may have been too close to the situation to see it objectively.

Journaling allows you to step back and, almost from a third-person perspective, relive the experience through different eyes. This can be your opportunity for a life- changing transformation.

Creating Your Legacy of Love

You may be documenting your personal relationship with the intention of keeping it for yourself. However, I have found that these journals make for wonderful family keepsakes, something to be passed on and to be cherished as a legacy of love. What I wouldn't give to have my Grandma Rose's handwritten memories of Ginger, our family Boxer and the first dog I ever encountered. I was just two years old at the time, and though I certainly remember the love of that dog, I wish I had more of Ginger's de-Tails! That would be a keepsake to pass on to future generations, a slice of my history. I encourage you to keep this in mind.

About Grief and Grieving

I know you might be anxious to jump into the journal but hang on. First we need to talk some specifics about grief, including what grief is, who grieves, some of the experiences that you may encounter along the path, some of the "myths" about grief and recommended ways to assess and work through them.

Grief Is Normal

Grief is an organic part of who we are as 2-leggers; it's a normal human response that awakens when there is sadness, a change, or a loss. This can be anything from the death of a loved one to the loss of a job, from the breakup of a marriage to the loss of a friendship. And these are just some of the most well-known examples. When studying for my grief certification, I learned about the different types of grief. Did you know that there are over forty-three? Even when the change is a happy one – such as the purchase of a new home – we may grieve the loss of the old.

Who Grieves?

Everyone grieves, no exceptions. Grief does not discriminate by gender, race, education or age. Even our pets grieve! We will cover that shortly; for now, suffice it to say that everyone will experience grief to various degrees at different times in their life.

People and Pet Grief

Is there a difference between grieving the loss of a person and the loss of a pet? *Should* there be a difference? This is somewhat of a sticky, even polarizing topic.

Pet parents report feeling embarrassed about their grief. They're afraid they'll be viewed as the weirdo's and that others will make them feel they don't *deserve the right* to mourn the loss of their 4-legger family member.

Given these very legitimate fears, grieving pet parents often feel like they don't have the outlet for their emotions. So what do they do? Isolate and bury their grief. Pet loss grief has been kept on the sidelines for way too long! Even well-meaning family and friends say, "You can always get another dog or cat or bird." They may even ask you right away when you are going to get another, as if your lost loved one was replaceable! People would never say such a thing if you had lost a 2-legger family member, though, truth be told, they do say some other insensitive stuff. Sometimes people simply don't know what to say to someone who is grieving, which is why when in mourning it's so important to find a tribe who understands.

Pet parents are definitely treated differently than others going through the grieving process. This, despite research that shows that pet loss can be just as devastating, if not more so, than losing a person.

Why? What causes these deep emotional bonds? Two words: *unconditional love*. We've all heard the term, but what does unconditional love really mean? What does it look like?

My market research background led me to seek out more information, and for this I turned to the people who understand unconditional love more than anyone else I know. It's now time to…

ASK THE PACK!

The Paws to Celebrate Pack described unconditional love as…

- "Love without stipulations or expectations"
- "Complete acceptance, pure love"
- "No judgement, *ever*"
- "Always happy to see you"
- "They can feel your emotions and will never abandon you"

What would you add to this list?

____

____

____

____

____

____

I don't know about you, but, I'm not so sure I can say the same things about many of the 2-leggers I know!

Most importantly, unconditional love does not discriminate. It doesn't care if someone has two, three, or four legs – or none at all - as long as it has a heart.

Children and Grief

Are there children in your life? Are you a parent, grandparent, maybe an aunt or uncle? Sometimes adults underestimate the awareness kids have around loss. Whatever your family unit looks like, remember that its littlest 2-leggers grieve as well!

Helping Heal the Child's Heart

Next to a grandparent, pet loss is usually a child's first experience with death. As a parent you have the opportunity to make this a healthy learning experience, rather than one that shocks them later in life.

There are so many factors to consider when this conversation takes place, for example, the child's age, how precocious/aware he/she is for their age, and whether there are older siblings who can help him/her understand. You might also take into account the age of the pet and whether they have already passed, or the end is approaching. Are you preparing your child for the loss or consoling them over one that has already occurred?

In most cases, when a pet passes, honesty is the best policy. The question remains however, how much *up-front, in your face* honesty is necessary or prudent?

Again, in making this decision you will want to consider the child's age and how life aware he or she is. As the parent or caregiver you are the best judge; just know that this can be a process of trial and error at the very least, and most definitely a test of your patience. As you will see from the story below, I have learned these lessons the hard way.

Precocious, Oh, I Think So...

I remember like it was yesterday, the day my two-and-a-half-year-old daughter asked me about sex. One minute I was going about my business, the next this tiny person was bluntly asking, "Did you and Dad ever do it?" I nearly fell out of my skin! I had to ask her to repeat what she'd said because I wasn't sure I had heard correctly, and boy was I hoping I hadn't!

"I want to know about sex," she demanded, "Did you and Dad ever *do it*?"

As the competent parent that I *thought* I was, I told her, "This is not the time for talking about this, we will do it later."

In my frazzled mind, I had just bought myself some time. After the kids went to bed, I would tell my husband what Dani had said and get his take on how we should handle it.

Well, I didn't get that opportunity. At dinner the same night, she decided that later meant *now.* With absolutely no trepidation, she looked at me, pulled herself out of her booster seat and away from the dinner table, and asked, "Okay, are we going to talk about sex now?"

My husband choked and looked at me. I shook my head and said, "What am I going to do?"

Knowing our daughter as we both did, we decided I'd better tell her something; otherwise there would be no end of these questions - questions I'd thought I would be able to avoid for at least another decade.

We headed up to my bedroom, and after she had made herself comfortable she announced, "I'm ready for sex-talk!"

I felt my blood pressure rising as I tried to construct the most basic response I could get away with. Thankfully, I was able to skirt around the anatomical parts, and after minimal questioning Dani seemed satisfied with my explanation that a mommy and daddy share their love for each other with some hugging and kissing. I was relieved. My husband was relieved. We had really dodged a bullet!

A few weeks later, however, we totally blew it when Dani's hamster Sophie died. We told the children that she had escaped into the basement and we had never been able to find her.

Fast forward. my daughter, now in her twenties, told me, "You have no idea how scared I was to go in the basement after Sophie died! I thought I was going to find her dead, rotting and decayed corpse down there. I never wanted to go in the basement again!"

What did I learn here? That my daughter would have been better off hearing the truth (or some softened version of it) about Sophie's death. Just as I'd done with the sex conversation, I should have taken into account what level of honesty she was capable of handling. I had to wait a long time to learn this lesson, but better late than never, right? At least I can now share it with you. Know what your child is capable of handling. Take it slow, make it simple, and be prepared for follow-up questions.

Your religious and spiritual beliefs will potentially come into play. It is entirely up to you to tell the child about Heaven and/or The Rainbow Bridge. I leave that entirely up to you.

I have found that once a child reaches age five or six they can comprehend more - and are curious about death; they also benefit from closure when they are allowed to participate. Nowadays, many parents include the children on their pet's final journey. It becomes a loving ritual where they can say their last goodbyes.

I believe each one of us holds the "heart of a child" – that is, the inner child living within us. Many people forget how to be playful and carefree as they grow up, but it only takes one furry, finned or feathered friend to awaken that inner child again. Similarly, when a pet passes, that child needs compassionate attention and nurturing to find recovery. Describing it here and in this context sounds a lot like the personality of grief, which we will come to very soon.

Just as you would comfort a little boy or girl after the loss of a pet, it is important to find ways to provide comfort to your inner child to help him or her pass through this grieving process.

Here is a bedtime story you can read to a “child” of any age to bring them comfort. I call it a Paws “Fairly Tail” of Faith.

The Tail of the Mending Heart

When our beloved transitions to the next step of their journey, they take a piece of our heart with them. And in its place, they leave a piece of their heart for us.

What most people don't realize is that the heartache of grief is the mending of two hearts fusing together as one!

As we work through our grief, the pain becomes more of an ache, allowing for smile breakthroughs when sweet memories of our times together appear.

Why do they take half of my heart and leave half of theirs? What is the purpose?

Because your beloved is watching over you, guiding you and they need a highly efficient and effective mechanism to keep track of everyone and everything back home on Earth!

And when the day comes for you to meet again, a message of love goes out to your beloved that your arrival is imminent and to get ready for your reunion!

Until then, you can always check that this equipment is working (because it is working, day and night, 24/7!). How? Easy, place your hand over your heart. Do you feel the gentle beat? That's your tracking device, your love connection until the day you meet again.

Do Pets Grieve Their Furry Siblings After They Die?

When our beloved pet dies, are we 2-leggers alone in our grief? What happens in households with multiple pets? What do the surviving "siblings" experience? Do they grieve? Do they mourn? Do they show signs of depression?

SCIENCE ALERT!!!

An article in Psychology Today cited the following study that was conducted in Australia and New Zealand in 2016 by Jessica Walker and her team.

Walker's sample was comprised of 311 pets - 159 dogs and 152 cats who live in a household with other animals and where one of their sibling pets had recently died.

Using what would be considered normal, common behaviors of grieving humans, researchers looked at the same behaviors among these 311 pets. Let's look at the chart below.

Behaviors Observed	**Dogs (159) %**	**Cats (152) %**
A sense of loss, looking for the sibling in places they would rest or nap	60	63
Clinginess - neediness	61	62
Vocalizing - whimpering	27	43
Appetite changes; increase/decrease	35	31
Sleeping increases	34	20

Overall, the findings show that for the most part, dogs and cats grieve the same, the exception being that cats are much more likely to communicate sadness through whimpering and whining than dogs (43% and 27%, respectively). On the other hand, 1 in 3 (34%) more dogs were observed sleeping for longer periods of time throughout the day, compared to only 1 in 5 (20%) cats.

Additional findings indicate that dogs seem to show an equal amount of grief-related behavioral changes regardless whether the animal companion they lost was a cat or another dog.

Researchers also wanted to know whether animals who had the opportunity to view, sniff and smell their deceased siblings' body would experience closure - in other words, would they understand that their companion was no longer alive and not coming back? In the study, 58 percent of the dogs and 42 percent of the cats got to view the body of their companion. The majority (73 percent) took the time to sniff and investigate their deceased sibling. However, no one reported behavioral differences between the animals who saw and/or smelled their companion's body and those who did not.

Researchers did conclude, however, that dogs act very much like human children younger than four, in that they do not have a concept of death as a final. Instead, they simply feel the loss of the presence, friendship, and companionship of their loved one; that loss causes their stress and grief-like behaviors.

The conclusion to draw from this study is that dogs and cats suffer from stress when a companion animal from their household dies. Because of this, they show behaviors which can be interpreted as grief. Furthermore, a dog is just as likely to grieve over the loss of the household cat as it is for the loss of a companion dog.

Helping Your Pets Grieve

Here you are, grieving the loss of your beloved pet and now you also need to lend comfort and support to the remaining members of your fur family. What do you do?

There is a bit of a language barrier here, but you still need to maintain the "alpha" position. You need to *show and tell.* Speak to these loved ones in a firm, calming, reassuring tone. Facial expressions are read by our pets, so be sure your face and words are in synch with each other. I encourage you to talk to your pet about their sibling who's passed, speaking their name can provide comfort. Another recommendation when you "run out" of things to say, read to your pet. Any book will do, but I'm a fan of children's books for this purpose! Take your love for a one-on-one cuddle-fest and read aloud. The sound of your loving voice and the warmth of your snuggle-connection is very healing…for both of you!

Spending time with family is more important now than ever. Consider an extra walk, extra fetch, or other pleasant outdoor activities. You may find this to be mood-lifting for all.

Just as we 2-leggers have a tendency to "eat our feelings" when sad or depressed, be conscientious of extra treats for the fur family. Their long-term health resides with you.

Like 2-legger grief, it does not happen overnight, there is no set timeline in pet sibling grief. They will recover and heal in their own way and time, just as we do. Remember, no matter how long it takes to heal, everyone's relationship is unique and deserves patience and respect.

Guilt: The Unwanted Passenger

As I've mentioned previously, not all grief is the same; in fact, it's unique and complicated. To help illustrate some of the elements of grieving, I'd like to share a personal revelation I encountered while on my journey. It was when I realized I was carrying that sneaky stowaway: guilt.

Goldie, Grief and Guilt: Part One

In the early days of our marriage, my husband Lou and I lived in an apartment. The building did not allow dogs, which for me, who had been pet-deprived as a child, was a real bummer. Cats were permitted however, and with the encouragement of my sister Lisa I decided to shop for a kitten. This, despite the fact that like my mother, I was extremely allergic (back then I referred to it as a "sensitivity," but who was I kidding?), and the fact that my husband had said he didn't want any pets. I didn't even tell him I was doing this; I wanted a kitten, and *nothing* was going to stand in my way.

She was a tiny tortoise-shell-colored kitten with a gold spot on her head, so I named her Goldie. When my husband arrived home that night, I happily announced, "Look what we have!"

There she was, a complete nut job chasing after a crumpled up empty cigarette package (I used to smoke three packs a day, which provided Goldie with endless hours of fun!). My husband looked at the kitten then me, his brow furrowing.

"I told you no pets," he growled, "Didn't you hear me say no pets?"

Yes, he was mighty peeved at me for getting her without talking to him first, but my heart was so happy I didn't care. He soon caved in and fell in love with this crazy kitten who was so much like a dog. For example, if we threw the crumpled cigarette package, she'd chase after it and bring it back to us over and over again. And if there was an empty brown grocery bag on the floor, Goldie would fetch and then deposit the cigarette package into the bag! She was also an "attack kitty." When anyone other than me or my husband came into the house, Goldie would bite at their ankles and run. She was a riot.

But I was definitely allergic to her. Oftentimes I would have to sequester myself in the bedroom, which was off limits to her. She hated being away from me, and she'd scratch at the door, begging for admittance. I can still hear those claws and meowing desperately trying to get in. Many times, I'd go out to be with her in order to keep my bedroom cat-dander-free.

I was as attached to Goldie as she was to me, and gladly bore the suffering, even when I developed asthma and had to use an inhaler. In my book, a lack of oxygen was a small price to pay to have this fluff ball of love.

This went on for nearly two years until I got the news: I was pregnant! I was over the moon, especially since I'd had an ectopic pregnancy the year before which required emergency surgery to remove my left fallopian tube. The doctors were unsure I would ever be able to get pregnant with one tube, but I did! It was like a miracle.

In the meantime, I had continued to use the inhaler and other assorted over the counter allergy meds. Finally, I had to come clean to my OBGYN about the array of medication I was taking, and he wasn't too happy about the frequent use of the inhaler. He recommended that I either stop the inhaler or rehome the cat.

This presented me with a catch-22. I couldn't continue the inhaler while pregnant and I couldn't breathe without it. After a long conversation with my husband, it was decided that we would find a good home for our Goldie. My heart was breaking. I was giving up my baby for my baby. It just wasn't fair!

Fortunately, I was able to find her a good home. An employee of mine told me his mother had recently lost her cat and he felt that Goldie would be a perfect match for her. It felt as right as it could feel, under the circumstances.

I will never forget the day my employee came to take her. As he picked her up and put her over his shoulder, Goldie looked back at me and my husband in utter confusion - at least this is what I intuitively felt.

When the door closed behind them, my husband and I burst into tears. I had never experienced a pain like this, and my husband, a big tough guy, became overwrought with emotion. Our lives had changed that moment, but we rationalized the pain away, telling ourselves that there was nothing we could have done differently. We were having a baby and it wasn't healthy for me to be using the inhaler during my pregnancy. This became our mantra for days, then weeks and almost right up to the day our son Jon was born.

As I look back at the time, I realize, I was *symbolically* euthanizing Goldie. She was rehomed, yes, but out of my life for good. Like all mothers I adored my new baby, but what I didn't realize until that moment was that I had unfinished grief for Goldie living inside my soul. I felt so guilty about giving her up. *Why did I have to rehome her?* I continuously asked myself, *Why couldn't I have kept her and tried harder not to use the inhaler, or get one of those huge air purifiers that cost over a thousand dollars to see if that worked?* And, the worst was, *Why did I even get her?* I would live with this emotional roller coaster for many years to come.

Every now and then, I thought of Goldie, wondering if she is well, or if she was even alive. I never saw her or the employee who took her from us again.

Eventually, I learned to bury my grief. I threw myself into being a working mother, thinking that time and life would erase the pain and guilt. But time didn't take it away. It was still there, waiting to be acknowledged.

It wasn't until I began studying for my grief specialist certification that I would come to terms with this buried guilt-grief sandwich.

In order to heal, I had to take a good look at my choices at that time. Although Goldie didn't die as a result of my choice to rehome, it was a permanent life change, for her and for us. Many changes in life can trigger grief and guilt. Let's review why.

One, I brought a cat into my life knowing full well that my husband did not want me to do it. Secondly, I was allergic, not the best logic on my part. Third, I had to rehome her for the health of my unborn baby.

What I learned is that we 2-leggers tend to use the word "guilt" in the wrong context. You may be calling what you're feeling guilt when it is really something else. If this is the case, you may be carrying this heavy burden unnecessarily, just as I did for many years with Goldie.

Dissecting this further, you need to ask yourself a few questions, such as, "Is there anything I wish I'd said or done differently? Are there some things I wish had happened better or more often?"

In my situation, I would answer, "Yes, maybe I should have never gotten Goldie." Then again, if I didn't, my husband and I would have missed out on all the happy moments that she gave us. Would I truly want to erase her from my memory? No, I wouldn't. However, what I could have or should have done is stay in touch with the employee and his mom to check on her welfare. It bothered me that I had never done this, but was I feeling *guilty*?

Guilt actually implies intent to harm. Now I had to ask myself, "Did I do anything with intent to harm Goldie?" Absolutely not! I knew in my heart that she deserved a loving home, to be taken care of by someone who would place her at the top of their priorities, and I had taken steps to ensure this. So is guilt the right word to use? No, the right word here is *regret.*

When you identify something you wish had been different, better, or more, you are on the path to understanding that what you really feel is not guilt, but unfinished or incomplete grieving with regard to your relationship with your pet.

Guilt, actual or imagined, feels like shackles tethering you to a painful place. It is also probably the most frequently cited emotion by pet parents. In order to heal and move forward, you must be able to remove those shackles. Identifying what you are truly feeling is the first step.

Let's examine another example of grief-induced guilt.

Guilt: Part Two

Aloneness allows for overthinking and second-guessing. Guilt can easily slip right in and take control if you let it.

Guilt should have no place in grieving. It makes you doubt your choices and if it has the chance, it will bring you deeper into a state of depression. In fact, I believe guilt to be depression's "second cousin."

Many of my clients discuss feeling "guilt" for two primary reasons, the first of which is what should rightfully be referred to as regret.

Statements of regret usually begin with, "Why didn't I…?" Sound familiar? "Why didn't I take her for more walks?"; "Why didn't I get that scratching tree?"; "Why didn't I take him to the ocean and play on the beach?"; "Why didn't we have ice cream more often?"

Chances are if you could objectively view that time, you would realize that you did go for many great walks. And the beach, you couldn't play on the beach because you live in a land-locked region, thousands of miles away from a body of water! The ice cream, okay, I kind of get that, as there are never enough opportunities for a good cone. The point I'm making is, what you call "guilt" is actually just your way of grasping for a human reason "why."

Let me remind you that at the time, you made the smart, responsible pet parent decisions. Do not question yourself. You can't change it or take it back. Living in the past prohibits you from moving into the future. Accept it.

The second common reason for pet parents' guilt - and this is the *big one* – is questioning your 2-legger right to make "that decision," the decision to euthanize.

I frequently hear, "Did I do enough for my pet? If only I saw the signs earlier. Why couldn't I save them? It was going to cost thousands of dollars that I don't have and there was no guarantee that they would live through the procedure! Was it really the time to let them go? If only, if I would have, could have or should have!"

I call this "2-legger brain babble", and with all due respect and love – STOP IT!

Asking the "what ifs" and "why didn't Is" is our human way of looking to find a reason for something that didn't end the way we wanted. When we cannot find someone or something to blame, we take a hard look in the mirror at ourselves and say, "Tag, you're it!" Somebody has to be at fault, and why not us, right?

Let me point out a few observations that I have made over the years as a pet loss grief professional, as well as a pet parent who has lost a fur baby or two.

Pet parents are usually laser-focused on their pet's needs - in many cases even more so than on their 2-legger family (just ask my husband, "What's-His-Name"). Pet parents are highly protective, intelligent, intuitive and trusting, and if you ask them, they'd say without missing a beat, "Hell, yes! I would take a bullet for my baby anytime!"

Pet parents are also some of the best untrained detectives and interviewers I've ever met. They know how to get information from their vet when their pet's health is in question.

So why second-guess yourself? Why doubt your judgement? Unless you were just a "spectator," sleeping your way through making healthcare decisions for your pet (which I highly doubt), you did what you could with the tools you were given. And, unless you are a trained vet with years of specialized education, you made choices by consulting with someone you trust, trained trust. Right?

Don't get me wrong, the decision to euthanize a pet is one of the toughest we will ever make. As I was told by my Paws Pack admin Cindy, those who grow up on farms see this as just a reality of life; for the rest of us, however, it is foreign and absolutely horrific.

But let's stop and think about this for a moment.

What if...maybe you could try to gamble for a bit more time with your pet, but who really benefits? Here, you must let the quality of your pet's life be your guide. If your pet will not recover to the point at which he/she will enjoy life, what is the point of putting them through a risky, invasive surgery? Sure, you might get a few more days or months, perhaps some more hugs, but your pet might also be experiencing more pain. There is also the exorbitant cost of surgery, which for many people may be a real issue.

When making this decision, lean on the person you have entrusted with your pet's wellbeing: your vet. Ask direct questions and be prepared for the answers you don't want to hear. Will an invasive surgery repair them and allow for many more good months and years? If the answer is no, then this is "the time." You are lovingly setting them free from pain and suffering.

Acceptance and Forgiveness

To heal, to get to the other side of grief, to forge our new normal, we need to accept that we cannot change the past; we can only deal with the here and now. Your other option is to live with this heavy burden dragging you down over an undetermined period of time. Think about it, it would be like carrying a backpack filled with heavy wet cement uphill with no end in sight. What do you gain from this? Self-punishment? This is not the way your pet would want you to live your life.

The following pet serenity prayer I created that has helped countless pet parents set down their burden and move forward. Mark it in the book, write it down on a sticky note, and repeat over and over again until it settles into your bones.

Pet Parent Serenity Prayer

I choose to accept and deal with it now, to take responsibility for the choices I made, acknowledge that at the time I made these choices and I took actions that were right for my beloved pet. And if in looking back, I feel it necessary to ask for forgiveness, that there is even a chance I did not make all the right choices, but I know in my heart and soul I made them with only the best intentions. I acknowledge it was never with intent to harm, therefore this is not guilt and I can now move forward with love in my heart.

Forgiveness is one of the last turns on your journey. You will be speaking to your pet through writing two letters. More de-Tails to come!

"Pet loss grief is a marathon of emotions that we complete for the one we love. It is the last Earthly gift we give. When you are feeling down, about to give up, remember who you are running this marathon for!"

-Pam Baren Kaplan

Stages and Phases

Now I would like to address something that I have heard from countless 2-leggers over the years. It goes something like this: "*Oh you're in the anger stage. It only feels like forever but soon you will be in the bargaining stage, not that its better but be prepared, the depression stage that comes after bargaining is a huge pain in the butt and then...*"

No.

Although there is a multitude of emotions that accompany loss, there are *no* set stages or phases of grief that neatly follow one to another.

It was once documented - and by very reputable sources - that there are five stages of grief: denial, anger, bargaining. depression and acceptance.

These five stages were developed by Dr. Elizabeth Kubler Ross and David Kessler, coauthors of *On Grief and Grieving,* which is widely considered to be the seminal book on the topic. Since then, Kessler has stated that they never intended these stages to represent a linier structure that neatly or even chronologically falls on a timeline, but in fact these are components or identifiers of what grief can contain. Yet to this day many of us 2-leggers continue to spout off about the "stages of grief."

Everyone's grief is unique, as is the way it manifests. That said, it is important for you to understand each of these five emotions so that you can better respond to the symptoms driving each response within your grief. Let's review them.

Denial

When we are in denial, we become numb. Even things that once gave us joy now seem meaningless. Thoughts float through our mind, such as "How do I go on? Why should I go on?" Everything is overwhelming and we look for ways just to make it through each day. But denial actually serves a purpose: it puts up internal roadblocks that help us manage the pace of grief, only allowing as much as we can handle at one time. Denial helps us cope and make survival possible.

As you become stronger and denial begins to fade, you may find yourself questioning your decisions around the loss, as well as your own life experience and all of the feelings you have been pushing down (denying). They will begin to rise to the surface, searching for your attention.

Anger

Anger is like a lit match to gasoline, flames spreading quickly to those that you care most about; family, friends or God. It could even be directed toward the loved one who passed and left you here to deal with this life alone. Anger is like a thick protective wall between you and your pain. Whereas denial feels like a paper cup in the wind - lost and untethered- anger hunts for a connection, a target. Anger is easily triggered by something that someone says or does. That is when you snap.

Now you have something to clutch onto, something tangible to connect the depth and strength of your anger. As scary as it can be, anger is a necessary emotion for healing, but you must be willing to work through it. The more you feel, the harder you work through it, and the more you heal.

Bargaining

"If you let Fluffy live, even just another year, I'll stop drinking, I won't swear anymore, I won't eat another carb...*ever*!" The list goes on and on.

This is bargaining. Before a loved one passes, we find ourselves making deals, negotiating with whoever will listen, hopefully someone with the powers of Divine Intervention. We say things, we pray, and we desperately beseech the heavens to spare us from this pain.

After the loss, the celestial bargaining turns into a somewhat unrealistic truce. For example, "What if I dedicate the rest of my life to charity, I'll donate my body to science..." all in the hopes of making everything right again, the way it was *before*. In essence, you're asking to step into a time machine and go back to change things, resulting in a totally different outcome. What it usually results in, however, is bargaining. That's when we find ourselves on the vicious loop of "What if I...?"; "Why didn't I...?"; "If only I...!" - also known as the woulda, shoulda, coulda's, or as I refer to this trio as, "The Triplets of Regret." As mentioned previously, we 2-leggers have an innate need to find the source of blame, and when we can't point a finger at others we'll put it on ourselves. We remain locked in that dance between bargaining and guilt – anything not to feel the pain.

Depression

Today, if you watch any commercial television, you are inundated with ads for pharmaceuticals to aid in the soothing of your depression. Depression is a normal response to grief! You are struggling through a great loss and there is deep sadness and feelings of emptiness. So many of these other emotions *hitch that ride* on grief, leading to moments of intense sadness, withdrawal from family and friends, questioning life and how to go on in a life without your loved one; these are just a few of the statements reported by those in the throes of depression.

All too often others see depression after a loss as *terribly wrong, out of control, it's something that has to be fixed. You must just snap out of it!* Pop an antidepressant, and if that one doesn't work let's try one of the many others on the market today.

Grief-induced depression is real and its *ruff;* in fact, the deeper and stronger your bond with your lost loved one, the longer and deeper the depression. To not experience some depression after a loved one dies would be unusual. When a loss fully settles in your soul, the realization that your loved one didn't get better this time and is not coming back is depressing. If grief is a process of healing, then depression is one of the many necessary steps along the way.

That said, if you were previously diagnosed with and/or are being treated for chronic depression, grief can definitely exacerbate it. Please work with your therapist and physicians for appropriate treatment.

Acceptance

As this is a commonly misunderstood term, I'd like to begin with what acceptance is *not*.

It is not giving in or giving up. It isn't "I'm okay and everything is alright despite the fact that I have lost my beloved family member!" (This, by the way, is denial.) The truth is, many people never feel "okay" or "alright" about the loss!

Acceptance *is* accepting that this is your new reality; you are living a life without your loved one in it and it's permanent. You don't have to like it but resisting becomes futile. Life will continue to move on with or without you, but much better for you if you accept that you need to forge *your* new normal.

Finding acceptance may mean having more okay days than bad ones. As we begin to start enjoying things again, we often feel like we are betraying our loved one. We can never replace our love, but we can make new connections and new meaningful relationships.

Acceptance means that instead of denying our feelings, we start listening to our needs; we change, we grow, we evolve. We may begin to reach out to others and become involved in their lives. We invest in our friendships and in our relationship with ourselves. We begin to live again, but we cannot do so until we have given grief its rightful time.

I encourage you to grieve and grieve completely. Do not fear these five, for they are a part of the process that grievers need to push through holistically and organically. They may follow in some order but, be prepared, you may find anger returns more than once during the grieving process, or that depression hangs on until acceptance. I cannot stress enough how important it is to walk this journey and take on the challenges to completing your grief. No holding it all in and try to bury it in busyness to avoid feeling. It's an easy option for some, but unfinished, unresolved grief becomes a sickness that settles in the soul. It manifests as deeper depression, and we know that depression will be an anchor attached to your spirit. Staying in bed with the covers over your head and imbibing in any other depression-induced bad behavior will most likely be more paralyzing than positive.

Hi,
my name
is Grief

Tending to the Personality of Grief

Nurturing

If we hope to be successful at getting through to the other side, each one of us needs to accept responsibility for tending to our own grief. Grief requires positive attention and nurturing. Left on its own, grief will act out and throw a tantrum until it gets the much-needed care and compassion.

Imagine grief as a small child within you, or it might be easier to think of it as a twelve-week-old kitten or puppy, just beginning to learn about life. You are to parent and gently teach your grief about love, and this begins by taking care of you.

Self-care / Self-love

Patience goes hand in hand with self-love and care. Give yourself some space, some breathing room. You have been through a great emotional upset. You will be encountering many changes in your regular routine and thought processes and, as I reiterate many times throughout this book, getting through to the other side does not happen overnight. It is a marathon, not a sprint! And again, remember who you are running this marathon for! Here are a few gentle but beneficial self-care recommendations:

- Try to stay on a regular schedule of rising and going to bed.

- Make your daily shower a healing ritual. Like myself, many of my clients find a warm/hot shower to be very soothing. Imagine the hot water washing the sadness and negativity away.
- Stretch, walk, do yoga, and receive massage therapy. When in emotional pain, your body tends to tighten or stiffen up. Be sure to get up and move every few hours. Seek a trained massage therapist to work out the knots and toxins that live in your muscles. It is healing, and it feels so good!
- Nourish yourself with healthy foods and beverages.
- Smile. Research shows that our brains can be tricked into a healthier mind and body. Have you ever heard, "Fake it till you make it?" It applies here and there is science to back that up! Smiling can trick your brain into believing you're happy, which can then spur actual feelings of happiness. But it doesn't end there.

SCIENCE ALERT!!!

In a 2017 article for NBC New, Nicole Spector cites Dr. Murray Grossan, an ENT-otolaryngologist in Los Angeles, who points to the science of psychoneuroimmunology (the study of how the brain is connected to the immune system), which asserts that depression weakens your immune system. Happiness, on the other hand, has been shown to boost our body's resistance.

"Just the physical act of smiling can make a difference in building your immunity," states Dr. Grossan. "When you smile, the brain sees the muscle [activity] and assumes that humor is happening."

In a sense, the brain is a sucker for a grin. It doesn't bother to sort out whether you're smiling because you're genuinely joyous or because you're just pretending.

"Even forcing a fake smile can legitimately reduce stress and lower your heart rate," adds Dr. Sivan Finkel, a cosmetic dentist in New York City.

A study performed by a group at the University of Cardiff in Wales found that people who could not frown due to Botox injections were happier on average than those who could frown. (Hmmm? Happiness and wrinkle-free? I think I see the connection!) Though this sounds great, smiling doesn't cost anything, and you don't need a prescription!

"When the right time is here,
the right love will appear."

-Pam Baren Kaplan

Triggers and Emotional Responses

Getting through to the other side takes preparation and practice. Remember, running this marathon leads to your recovery. So how do we "go the distance?" How do we see this through? Let's get some things out on the table, okay? Okay!

Crying

Crying is a normal response to sadness. Like grief, crying does not discriminate; it's an equal opportunity emotional response and, lucky us, we are the only mammals (at least the only ones scientists know of) that shed emotional tears!

Science Alert!!!

Tears are primarily made up of water but behave differently. There are three different types of tears we 2-leggers produce: reflex, continuous and emotional tears.

Reflex tears help your eyes clear the "stuff" that you might encounter throughout the day: pollution, pet dander, makeup, a passing insect, etc.

Continuous tears keep your eyes moisturized to do their usual normal job. Blinking would be a real pain in the butt if we didn't produce these continuous tears!

Emotional tears are different. They contain stress hormones, which explains why researchers believe that crying emotional tears actually helps relieve stress. Just one of the many benefits of crying! Now let's dive into some of the others.

The Seven Benefits of Crying

1. Detoxes
   - Lubricates our eyes to work normally
   - Releases some stress hormones
   - Are an exit plan for the junk we get in our eyes
2. Emotionally soothing
   - Crying may be one of your best mechanisms to self-soothe. Researchers have found that crying activates the parasympathetic nervous system (PNS). The PNS helps your body rest and digest. The benefits aren't immediate. It may take several minutes of shedding tears before you feel the soothing effects of crying.

     This is a little more science to backup just how amazing tears are, and a legitimate comeback to the "dumb stuff" people may say!

     The next time somebody says, "Would you just get over it and stop your crying!", you can confidently look them right in the eye and announce that you are in a "self-soothing", healing mode, it's a scientific fact, and they can just "shove it." Or, maybe you just walk away from them blowing your nose but feeling mightily empowered with knowledge!
3. Dulls pain

- Crying for long periods of time releases oxytocin and endogenous opioids (aka endorphins).
- Those *feel-good* chemicals can help ease physical and emotional pain.
- Once the endorphins are released, your body may go into somewhat of a numb stage, giving you a sense of calm or well-being.

4. Improves the mood

- Along with helping you ease pain, crying, specifically sobbing, may even lift your spirits.
  - When you sob, you take in many quick breaths of cool air.
  - Breathing in cooler air can help regulate and even lower the temperature of your brain.
  - A cool brain is more pleasurable to your body and mind than a warm brain. As a result, your mood may improve after a sobbing episode.

5. Interpersonal benefits

- When you are sad, crying is a way to let those around you know you are in need of support. This is known as an interpersonal benefit.
- A baby's crying has been referred to as attachment behavior. Its function is in many ways to obtain comfort and care from others.
  - This helps to build up your social support network when the going gets tough. You learn who your friends are during times like this!

6. Grief recovery

- Grieving is a process.
- Crying as we have been discussing here, may even help you process and accept the loss of a loved one.

7. Restores emotional balance

- Crying doesn't only happen in response to something sad. In fact, you may cry when you are extremely happy, scared, or stressed.
- Researchers at Yale University believe crying in this way may help to restore emotional equilibrium. When you're incredibly happy or scared about something and cry, it may be your body's way to recover from experiencing such a strong emotion.

Bonus Benefit!

Grieving pet parents cry a very special type of tear, I call this "liquid love," and in my opinion, that alone should legitimatize your tears.

Crying Disclaimer!

As with grief itself, the length of time one allows themselves to cry will vary; however, if after a few days or a week the crying has not lightened, if it continues to invade your day-to-day routine and you find yourself feeling so depressed you don't want to get out of bed or your meals consist of a half-gallon of ice cream and you find yourself isolating from your loved ones, I recommend you seek medical advice. And if you *ever* feel like you want to hurt yourself or others, immediately (In United States) call The National Suicide Prevention Lifeline at: 1-800-273-8255

For readers outside of the US, please check within your country for suicide prevention resources.

Fatigue

Grief is exhausting. Your body will feel as if you have completed a 26K and, as I've shared, in many ways you have been through and will continue to forge ahead in a marathon of physical, emotional and spiritual upheaval.

If you are a heavy coffee drinker or sports energy beverage consumer, now is a good time to cut down and allow yourself the opportunity for much-needed rest. The mind needs to quiet or take a break from all this thinking. I also find that meditation works well at bedtime. There are many great meditation apps available to choose from. If that doesn't work for you, my clients recommend soft music, audio books or podcasts read by a soothing voice or just total silence in a cool dark room that can relax your brain and allow sleep to take over. If you tend to fall asleep to the TV, this may be working against you. Try turning it off for a few nights and experience the silence and darkness; you may get more restful sleep.

Try to stick to a regular routine; this includes both napping and a consistent bedtime each night. If you find yourself napping either too frequently or for too long a time, this may be impacting your ability to fall asleep for the entire night. Try cutting the frequency or lengths of your naps.

Preventing Dehydration

This is always important to good health but even more so when grieving. Drink plenty of water at this time. I *do not* recommend alcohol. Primary reasons; alcohol will most likely cause depression and can act as a diuretic, depleting essential vitamins and minerals. Overall, water is the best fluid to replace the fluids from tears. And a good multivitamin wouldn't hurt either.

Socialize – Interaction with Family, Friends and Co-Workers

One of the last things that people in grief want to subject themselves to is social gatherings. Grievers want to hibernate, to isolate and not engage with others for long periods of time. They prefer to be alone than worry about dodging the comment of the well-meaning, the not-so-well-meaning and the never-well-meaning (aka the bullies).

Enter the Pet Loss Crusader

I remember the first time the "pet loss crusader" was awakened. It was the early 90s, and I was working for a market research company managing a call center that employed a couple hundred people: housewives, moonlighters and my most favorite of all, teenagers. I shudder even to think about it.

We were the annoying people who called you at six p.m., just as you were about to sit down to dinner. Your phone would ring and there would be one of my employees trying to get you to answer forty-five minutes of survey questions on feminine hygiene products or adult diapers. Chances are you hung up, but not before uttering a few choice words. That was the reality of my life back then.

As the manager of what I lovingly referred to as an "over-sized day care center," I was in charge of all the personnel issues. Employees would call out, come in inebriated or with personal problems they needed to work out.

One employee, who I will refer to as "Gail," came into my office crying. She sat down with tears in her eyes, grabbing a fistful of tissues from the box on my desk and began to explain that her family dog had died, and she needed a few days off for bereavement. A supervisor was in my office at the same time and upon hearing her request let out a loud snort. I remember turning to the supervisor and snapping, "Hey, be quiet!", but my words fell on deaf ears.

"You're asking for time off because your doggie died?" he asked in this sing-song sarcastic tone? "I can't believe what a lame excuse that is to take off from work!"

Gail began to sob uncontrollably. Never having had the experience of losing a pet, I could only imagine what this pain was like. I felt anger rising up from my gut and I yelled, louder than I should have at the supervisor, "Who do you think you are?" I even startled myself! I then told him to get out of my office and I would deal with him later. I wanted to console my employee.

Unsolicited, she began to tell me her story. The words were flying out without as much as a pause for air. It was as if these were her last words on Earth and, by God, she was going to tell me. Between nose blows and fresh tissues, I learned just how much this dog meant to her. This was her childhood dog; she had told him every secret, more than she had shared with her family and few friends, to whom she never felt close enough or trusted. This dog never laughed at her like her siblings did. This pup loved her no matter what and she loved him right back. Her heart was so broken, I could almost feel the pieces coming apart.

She cried for a few moments without trying to speak, and then she said, "Thank you for letting me tell you this, I really appreciate you not laughing or judging me."

I asked her if I could give her a hug. Back in those days the issues of sexual harassment were just coming to light, so I figured better safe than sued.

She gladly accepted my hug. I told her that she may take off two days to mourn her pup. As she was getting up to leave, I realized I didn't even know her dog's name, so I asked, "Gail, before you go, what is this love's name?"

She stopped and smiled at me and said, "His name was Bugs, I named him after the cartoon. Thank you so much for asking and caring. I feel a little better now." Then she left my office.

I carried that experience with me. I never forgot just how fragile Gail was, and to witness this type of bullying was completely uncalled for. That moment was an awakening, the birth of a very different mindset that would set me on the path to my life's purpose.

When it comes to any social involvement, start slowly; attempt to surround yourself with others who are compassionate and understand your grieving and do not judge you or try to push you through this very personal process at their pace.

I have found that a lot of 2-leggers are inadequately educated with consoling someone in grief, let alone those going through the loss of a beloved pet. Which leads me right into…

Navigating Around Well-Meaning People

And today, we have an installment of, "The Dumb Stuff People Say!"

Has this ever happened to you?

A well-meaning friend, lost for words, is trying to be consoling and instead offers meaningless platitudes?

"He'll be okay, he's in a better place."

You might be thinking that, "*He," was never going to be okay again, and in what better place are you referring to?*

Hang on, here's another beauty…

Even some so-called experienced grievers aren't sure what to say to you. They too end up uncomfortably babbling on and not realizing that they are actually saying something hurtful, inappropriate, or just plain dumb. For example, "Be strong, I know exactly how you are feeling."

Be strong? Be strong for who? And how can you truly know

"exactly" how I'm feeling? This can incite more anger from the griever.

How do you deal with this? How can you navigate through these comments and not make a bad situation worse? Okay, you have choices… yes, you really do. You can…

1. Ignore the dumb comment

2. React and potentially start a battle you really don't want to fight at this particular time.

3. You can respond. What's the difference between reacting and responding? Reacting is knee-jerk, battle-igniting behavior, whereas, responding is mindful and stands a better chance of shutting down the dumbness. Responding is an art that needs careful practice and absolutely no alcoholic beverages consumed in the previous hour.

So, how *do you* respond?

The key word here is briefly. Saying something like, "Thank you for your concern" or "I appreciate your thought" and walk away. Do not get trapped trying to convert or educate anyone during your time of mourning. Keep it short and sweet, then muster up a small smile and walk away.

Now, what if you find yourself in the position of consoling the griever? Here's a few tips on doing so with sensitivity and compassion.

1. When you don't know what to do, just be present with the griever; keep an arm's-length distance to respect personal space.
2. If you're at a loss for words, it's okay to tell them you are searching for the right words to say but having a hard time coming up with them.
3. Do express that you care about them, love them and are here for them.

That's the comfort and support a person in grief needs.

"You Can Always Go Get Another"

This is a good time to address that unsolicited comment heard by countless grieving pet parents around the world. Remember, not everyone understands what you are experiencing, especially those who have never had a loving relationship with fur-family. Even those who were one-time pet owners may have very different beliefs. I look at the companion animal-to-human bond on a spectrum of sorts; there are all different levels of attachment and personal investment, from pet fanatic to barely engaged. Yes, these 2-leggers exist, and a variety may even live within the same household with you!

Maybe you know "that" person who thinks they know everything there is to know about pets? They claim to know the best solution for everyone else. Here's the scenario…

A friend sits you down to share from their own life experiences. Okay, here it comes…

"When I was a kid, my dog died. Well of course I was sad! But my folks went right out to that pet store and bought me another dog! That's what you need to do! Absolutely! I'll even drive you there!"

Yes, I agree that they are attempting to be compassionate, helpful in their own way, but it doesn't set with you, doesn't feel quite right with you. What do you do?

Thank them for their advice, you will be taking all of this in and then, politely excuse yourself and walk away. It's a lesson in, Pick Your Battles 101.

For some, that may be a solution, but as cliché as it sounds, one size doesn't fit all. Many of my Pack and personal friends who do rescue feel it is a tribute to the pet that passed to immediately go out and adopt - not shop but rescue an animal. "Give another their fur-ever home!" While this is a very noble thing to do, it has to be right for you.

Whether we've experienced a 2 or 4-legger loss, I believe that we need to allow a time to grieve and mourn, time to reflect on what this life has meant to you, a time to celebrate and to heal. It's an act of love as well as respect. But, right time or not right time, it has to bode well with you. When might that be? Could be a week, a few months, or maybe even a year.

"When the right time is here, the right love will appear."

I remember well the emptiness in our home when Roxy passed. It was like the color had drained from my life; it was a void in my spirit. I missed what our life was together. The depression seemed to emulate the never-changing days from the film Groundhog Day. Every day was like the day before until the change was meant to happen.

How will you know? Your gut starts talking to you, your intuition connects. It is kind of spiritual, but you'll find that your heart and mind are finally in agreement. Here's what happened to me…

Getting Zuzu

The morgue-like emptiness of our home wasn't getting better; it wasn't enough. Although torn between grieving our Roxy and the desperate ache for warm, doggie cuddles and canine craziness, we came to a very difficult family decision that we would, "look into" adopting a puppy.

The family agreed it would be another Lab, but per my daughter's demand, no yellow. We would never replace Roxy! My

Dani was having a much more difficult time with the idea of getting a dog. She was still grieving over her sister, her best friend in the entire world, the only soul with whom she had shared her most intimate secrets. No other dog would ever be allowed into Dani's heart.

I felt differently. In fact, after a great deal of time-consuming research on Lab breeders in the Northern Illinois and Southern Wisconsin area, I felt my mood lifting for the first time since Roxy's passing.

That's not to say I didn't understand what Dani was feeling. At first, I too felt as if I was betraying my girl. But then I spoke to Roxy.

"Rox," I said, "you know how sad we have been since you passed and that I will never, ever, ever, never replace you! You're my first baby and you will always be the primary tenant of mama's heart! We need your help and guidance, could you send us a puppy, the right puppy and at the right time, one that you'd approve of?"

I repeated this prayer-request many times over the next few months.

Late in the summer of 2011 we decided to adopt a chocolate Lab puppy from Thunder Labradors in Edgerton Wisconsin. After a pre-visit to check out the breeder and his dogs, it was a done deal. On Gotcha Day, September 14, the fam set out on an adoption road trip.

We had the first pick of five females. I remember it was a cold windy day and we were outside with five, seven-week old bundles of chocolate fluff. They were all so cute. But one was a little different than the others; she was more independent and even a little aloof. When I picked her up she was licking my face, put a paw on my cheeks and told me, "I'm the one, take me."

And it was decided. This little one was named Zuzu in honor of my favorite holiday movie of all times, the one I start crying from every time I hear the words: "Look Daddy, every time a bell rings an angel gets their wings."

I'm a sap, I'm a huge marshmallow. No denial.

And home we went! Zuzu was a beautiful little package of puppy. So smart that upon coming home to her new life, she began scratching on the patio door, she had to go out! She never had an accident in the house. I was thanking Roxy for this perfect puppy. It really feels that Roxy had sent us the right one!

Puppies can fool you into falling in love with them; they rope you into all of that adorableness, but man, are they exhausting! Zuzu was a daytime maniac! Voracious chewer and destructor of all. On one of her first rides in my car, she chewed right through the seatbelt of my Audi TT convertible roadster! My daughter lovingly referred to Zuzu as the "emotional terrorist!"

She didn't chill until nine p.m., when she finally turned off for the night. Although a wild-child, Zuzu was the epitome of the silly

Lab. She would get on her back and wiggle all four legs in the air and throw toys up in the air and catch them in her mouth over and over again. This earned her the nickname the "Upside-down Brown Clown." Her antics caused so much laughter; they were beginning to fill some of the cracks left in my heart by her "big sister."

One day, while in a rare moment of Zuzu-calm, I noticed an odd chunk of yellow fur right at the base of her tail. Now I know it is possible for Lab litters to have more than just one color, but Zuzu's bio-mom was a chocolate and the entire litter was chocolate. What was this chunk of yellow doing there?

Smiling wide, I remembered my wish, the pre-Zuzu conversation with Roxy. I then showed my husband and said to him, "Go with me on this one. What if Roxy made this little girl for us, knowing how sad we were without her and sent her to us? This chunk of yellow is Roxy's signature or her stamp on Zuzu's butt before she pushed her down to us from heaven?"

When it comes to my way-out, spiritual regurgitations, my husband has learned to go with the flow: don't question it, just accept it and walk away. No debate today. I believe this little tail of Zuzu's to be evidence as her gift from the Bridge, a special delivery from Roxy. I will always be so grateful, thank you my love!

Practicing Grief Recovery

Time Heals All Wounds: Myth or Reality?

It's been said over and over since the beginning of time by well-meaning family, friends and strangers alike: *"Don't worry, sweetheart, just give it time. Time heals all wounds."*

This has some truth in it. But so much depends on how *productively* you use that time to move *through* grief. We will never really get *over* a loss, it is something that changes organically within us over time.

That said, time is where we do the work in order to heal. Now, it may seem that the word "work" has an unpleasant connotation and, truth be told, you have some *ruff* stuff to deal with. Some days you may feel like you're walking through three feet of snow, barefooted with a baby elephant on your back; other days it might seem you are on a hamster wheel with no sign of a finish point. *It's work!*

The Emotional Tidal Wave

You are investing your precious time to recover. You will undoubtably be facing the challenges of the emotional tidal wave head-on. Let's huddle and prepare to start your training.

Grief is erratic. There are so many feelings that come out of nowhere, rising and falling, like a tidal wave. Your focus must be on finding balance when the waves hit. Imagine your mission is to learn to ride these ruff waves, you learn to surf. Your strategy is to stay atop the surfboard when those high waves try to knock you off. You must hang on tight to get through those turbulent waters. This is not the time to consider letting go! Hold on with all your might! You are learning. Remember, you may fall off that board once or maybe ten times, and each time you must climb back on again. This requires courage as well as patience.

After what may feel like hours, the high tide recedes. But the more you practice, the better you will get at staying on the board. You will find yourself becoming stronger and more confident after each confrontation with the waves of emotion. You will begin to find balance. You will find yourself surfing!

A new normal is now being forged. You may realize that you are not the same as before, you have grown from this lesson of love and loss.

Worst Firsts

The first year following the passing of your loved one may be the hardest. Holidays, birthdays and family events that you shared together - everything and anything can trigger that emotional tidal wave.

Even good times are brutal, for you then remember that your loved one is not there to share them. It seems everything is tainted by your loss. You start to wonder if you will ever feel happy and whole again.

I caution you, these worst firsts can drop in anywhere, and at any time. For example:

You may be in your car and a song comes on reminding you of your love. ***Trigger!***

There may be a commercial on TV with a dog or cat that looks like your angel. ***Trigger!***

You may be in the grocery store and passing the pet food aisle. Perhaps you started heading down it, only to remember that you no longer need anything there. ***Big trigger!*** These are just a few commonly reported worst firsts.

Now you may be thinking, “Does this mean that after twelve lunar cycles my grieving will come to an end? That I will no longer feel the heartbreak?”

Unfortunately, the answer is probably not. However, over the year you will find that your extreme pain transitions into something like a dull ache. You are always aware of it, but you can learn to live with it for the rest of your life. Remember, grief never really goes away, it lives within us. It’s your love living in your heart.

Right Brain Activity and Healing

As we’ve discussed, time alone does not heal all wounds. You have to invest productively in your grieving. I believe that one of the most direct pathways to pet loss grief recovery is through right brain creative activity; namely, writing, drawing, journaling and sharing your stories and memories (or, as I like to call them, Tails).

Anything creative, including things like baking and cooking or decorating or redecorating a place in your home, can be a healing activity. I can’t tell you how many times I have rearranged rooms in my home when I get down! And it helps; it feels like I have a new place to go and find my creative side.

Another huge right-brainer is music! Music is a fantastic way to exorcise the sadness and stress out of your soul. No matter if it’s classic rock, opera, country or soulful blues, play that music loud and proud. Belt out a tune when no one is home or drive them crazy and maybe they will even join in! You’ll be amazed at how quickly it works its healing magic.

Creativity in any form exercises the right brain. Doing activities that allow the brain to relax, slow down and appreciate the act of creating something for and about your loved one is another step toward the other side of grief.

Check out the Section Three: Tools & Templates for *Making A Memory Garden*

Your Considerations

Order: Chronological or Random?

As the author of your story, you are in control over the topics and the order in which to write about them.

There may be topics that don't apply to your relationship; for example, if you rescued a dog that was a few years old, you can skip discussing the puppy years. No worries! We include extra pages for your personal topics in the Appendix called "My Tail Topics."

With regard to the order, you can choose to write chronologically or in random order. There is no right or wrong way to approach your journey. That said, I strongly encourage that you leave the love letters for last, as everything up to that point will help you prepare for them.

Voice

This is important. You decide whose voice or narrative perspective you are writing from. Some questions might feel right to come from your perspective, while others you may want to write from your pet's point of view. I leave this up to you! It may vary but be conscious of who "owns" the tail perspective.

Where Do I "Write?"

Whether you are using the print or e-version of the book, my thank you and free gift is a link at the back of the book to download all of the journaling pages.

Many of my clients like to use the journal pages as guides to make a Memory Book or a scrapbook where they can get really creative and incorporate all of their keepsakes in one book. I leave this up to you!

Mindfulness

I cannot stress enough to move at your own gentle pace. Grieving is a unique process, and for each person the length of time is different.

10 Recommendations to Minimize Emotional Exhaustion

Though deeply healing, journaling can take you on an emotional ride. This is the "ruff" stuff I've mentioned already. As you journal your way through your journey, you can use the following tools to minimize emotional exhaustion and find your balance.

1. Commit to an amount of time that you will devote to this journey each day or week. Be realistic and gentle with yourself in setting this goal.
2. Find a clean, comfortable, uncluttered place to do your work; you'll discover that you will get better results.
3. Some people prefer to work with music in the background, some prefer silence. Do what works best for you, keeping in mind that you can change it up depending on your mood that day. You make the rules!
4. Express yourself without censoring yourself. You are writing for you. No one else needs to read this love work, so write to your heart and from your heart!
5. Allow yourself freedom to create! If your inner kid wants to play, let him or her do so! Experiment with different writing and drawing mediums – markers or crayons; pencils or ink;

color or black and white - whatever you like working with. Find the fun in this journey.

6. Communicate in pictures!
   - Add photos or mementos of meaningful times and places.
   - Here is an example of what one client journaled about her dog's fast food experience.
     - The pup had his first ice cream cone and she captured a photo. She saved the ice cream cone wrapper and posted a picture of that messy event on her journal page. The wrapper was used as the background of the photo! Whenever my client looks back at this page, she smiles and feels a sense of connection with that moment. It's been said that "A picture is worth a thousand words!" In this case, maybe a million tears of love as well!
       - If you don't have or can't find a photo of a specific memory, re-create the moment! Take a photo of that important spot and use it to recall your tail!
       - You can also use the Vision Board method by cutting out images from magazines or newspaper to tell your tail!
7. Have you ever woken up remembering a dream, only to have it slip away a little while later? Or have you ever been in the grocery store line and a memory flashes by? These are telepathic text messages from your angel, tapping on your shoulder and whispering, "Hey, remember when we…?" You may want to keep a little pad and pen with you to capture these random thoughts that come to you at odd times and places.
8. Crying, as often and for as long as you need to, is highly encouraged. Keep a box (who am I kidding - a case!) of

tissues next to your workspace. As I like to say, *"If the sky can cry, so can I!"*

9. After you complete your work for the day, I highly recommend a ritual of transition back to the now. You do not want to "*wear*" this throughout the rest of your day. A warm bath or shower to wash the grieving away is a wonderful symbolic way to rejuvenate.
10. If at any point you need additional grief support, you can:
    - Contact me for a private session
    - Join Paws to Celebrate Pack, the Facebook Pet Loss Recovery Support group: www.facebook.com/groups/pawstocelebrate
    - Consult with your family physician for other resources

I remind you that the purpose of this journal is to draw on the memories of your life with your pet. With practice, the process of journaling will soften your grief and transform it into love. Not just any love, but unconditional love. Own this, my dear ones, for you have been blessed.

"A whole-life celebration of love"

A Celebration of Life

Here is the page to place your favorite photo of your beloved family member who is the subject of your labor of unconditional love.

Name:

____

Date of Birth or Adoption Date:

____

Date Passed:

____

Section Two

Your Journal Begins

Creating a Mind Map

Getting started has always been a challenge for me. I can stare at a computer screen without one word down and look at the time and realize that an hour has passed. I am a perfectionist and tend to overthink; then I get stuck. Does this happen to you?

My solution to what may feel like a monumental hurdle is to first take a deep cleansing breath, remind myself that this is a work in progress and give myself permission to be less than perfect. This is a challenge!

Once I've centered myself a bit, I then allow my brain to regurgitate what's sitting up front, right on top - no rules, just write! When I give myself the freedom to express, I find that other thoughts soon follow. It's really quite magical!

For this purpose, I like to use a method called Mind Mapping. This is a type of outline or graphic image that allows you to do a brain dump. It starts with one specific topic, usually placed at the center or very top of the page, which encourages additional or sub-thoughts and ideas to come forth. These will help you create the plot for your tails. There is no specific order or structure, just let it flow organically. The beauty of mind mapping is that this helps the thought processes get going and flowing to prepare you for each next step of your journal. Think of it as the warmup before the workout.

Now, let's get started!

On pages 210-211, there are two templates for mind mapping - grid and free hand. Many people prefer to work outside of the book; that way if they want to re-write they can do so and save the book for the final draft. That is perfectly okay!

Start by getting a piece of paper – lined or unlined, it doesn't matter. Write your pet's name or place a favorite photo of your pet in the center of the page.

Next, take that deep cleansing breath!

Now start writing down every feeling or descriptive word or phrase that comes to your mind about your pet. Try not to overthink what you're thinking! Just write!

Are thoughts coming slowly? Try a short break, a little distraction. Get up for a drink of water, a bathroom break, maybe you need a light snack or some rest? It's all okay! You can always add more words and phrases at another time, and there is a good chance you will, as this process is great for opening the floodgates!

Remember to keep a little pad of paper and a pen by your bedside and in your pocket or bag. Oftentimes the memories come when we least expect them, such as upon waking, while grocery shopping or stuck in traffic. (If you're driving, be sure to pull over and come to a complete stop before recording your memory.)

To help get you started, I've shared an example from my journal. Remember, this is just one of many ways to do this. Only you can decide which way feels right for you!

The Online Version - Here is the one I created on my computer with a program I owned from my days of teaching seminars. If you are tech-savy, you might enjoy this. There are plenty of free mind map options - just do a Google search for Free Mind Map Tools.

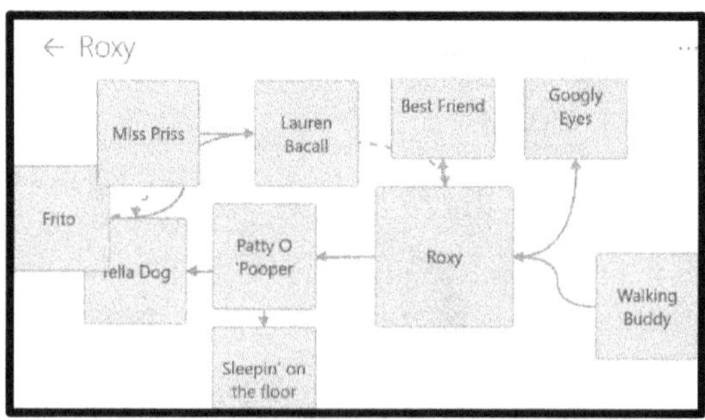

The Handwritten Version - Here is the mind map that I did by hand, can you tell? It's easy and, personally, I like to see the handwritten words, but this is your choice!

And, finally, the Grid Version

Pet's Name: Roxy

Silly girl	Yella
Big Appetite – Lab-Attite	Frito feet
Lays her head on my lap	Lauren Bacall
Scrunchy thief	Rodeo dog
Harvested her own peppers	Loved cherry tomatoes
Walkies	Bubb

The next step is to use your Mind Map to "Mind Map the Memories."

For each descriptive word or phrase that you recorded on your map, write a tail that explains your thoughts and feelings and brings the memory to life!

Don't worry if the words come slowly in the beginning. A few words can quickly become a paragraph; maybe that paragraph becomes an entire page! You can always start and come back to fill in more information at a later time. I am betting that you will!

This is work from the heart as well as the mind. In order to protect yourself from reliving the pain of your loss, you may be tempted to journal only about the happy times. Remember, though, that life is made up of a fantastic collage of experiences, both good and, well, not so good. They are tied together to form a life, your story. Healing requires you to experience it all, and journaling facilitates this. Do your pet – and yourself - justice and provide the *whole life tail.*

An Example of My Mind Map Memories: "Lauren Bacall"

We have a tendency in our family to attach characters from a film or TV show to the people and pets in our home. For example, Frankie, our youngest chocolate lab, is named for The Godfather's

"Frankie Five Angels" Pentangeli. Actually, we all have Godfather names - I am Tom Hayden, the wartime consigliere and my husband is the Don himself - but that's a tail for another time!

Back to Lauren Bacall…Rox was a beautiful, classy blonde broad with an attitude just like the movie star. Roxy was a loving Lab but could also be a little standoffish, just like a woman who is confident in her skin, or in this case, her own fur! She was model-gorgeous with a tiny hourglass figure right to the very end. I marvel at how beautiful she was in this picture my husband took of her when she was fifteen years young.

I always said, "Paws down, Roxy was and will always be the best and most beautiful yella dog ever."

It's now your turn!

Use the template page included in your book or take a separate piece of paper.

Follow the guidance on page 208.

Use a separate piece of paper for each word or phrase that you came up with. These are very important pages of your journal. *And remember, de-Tails please!*

A Pamism PawSpeak Acronym!

A̲lways

R̲emembered

F̲orever

Tail Pages

Each Tail Page provides "story starters" to help guide your way and shake loose some of those memories that haven't seen the sunlight in a while! You can use all of these starters, some of, or none!

If a topic does not relate to your relationship, no worries, this is about documenting your unique bond. Skip things that don't apply and work with pages that define your special love.

Be sure to add your own Tail Topics as well.

(See the "My Tail Topic List" and the template page provided on page 207. Work on any page, in any order that calls you.)

REMEMBER - Do not do the two letters until the other Tail Pages are completed!

Add pictures, paperwork, certificates, or trinkets to make your page come alive!

And above all, share the de-Tails!

Adoption aka "Gotcha Day"

What was the date I became yours?

How did you pick me or did I pick you?

What made me special?

Did I come from a rescue, breeder, pet store, or somewhere else?

Did you meet my "bio" Mom and Dad?

What were they like?

How many brothers and how many sisters were in my litter?

How much did I cost to "gotcha" me?

Who was there to bring me home?

What was my homecoming like?

How did I do that first night?

How Did I Get My Name?

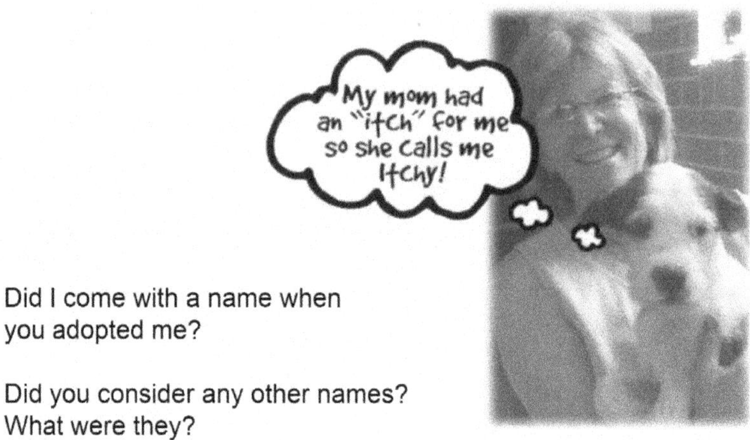

Did I come with a name when you adopted me?

Did you consider any other names? What were they?

Who came up with my name?

How quickly did I come when you called my name?

Nicknames Througout the Years

What were all of my nicknames?

How did I get them?

What was your favorite nickname for me?

PET

A Pamism PawSpeak Acronym!

Positive

Energy

Therapist!

Training Me!

Potty Training!

Tell me about my house-breaking history.

Did I pee or poop outside right away, or, was I a city dog with those indoor piddle pads?

How old was I when I stopped having "accidents?"

Did I have any weird bathroom habits or behaviors?

Crate/Kennel Training

Was I crate trained?

What did you call this place of mine? Crate? Kennel? Nest? What?

Did I sleep in my crate overnight?

How old was I when you allowed me full run of the house?

Did I ever sleep in your bed? If so, where was "my spot"?

Obedience Training

Did you take me to obedience classes, or did I have a “personal trainer”? Tell me about it.

Where did this training happen?

How did I do?

What did I do really well, and what took me longer to learn?

Did I make friends in class?

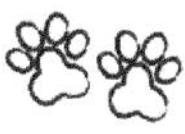

FOOD!

What was my relationship with food, did I wolf it down or was I finicky?

What pet food did you feed me?

Did I have a sensitive tummy or allergic to any food?

Who fed me?

What treats did I like?

Was I a beggar? If so, who "enabled" me?

My Favorite Toys

Did I like to play with toys?

What kind of toys were my favorite toys?

Was I a voracious chewer? Was I a fetcher?

Did I share my toys?

Getting Fixed
Neutered/Spayed

Was I already fixed when you gotcha'd me?

How young was I when I got spayed or neutered?

Did I have one of those silly, embarrassing cones to keep me from licking my stitches?

Was I a big baby or a brave little soldier?

Did my behavior change afterward?

WALKIES!!!

Did I like walks? Did you like walks?

Did I take you for a "pull?" Did I have a no-pull harness?

Was I my gracious charming self when we met up with other pups and their walkers?

Did we go on hikes?

Taking Photos and Fending Off the Pupparazzi

Was I a “cam-ham” or was I camera shy?

Pull out some favorite photos of me to put in this journal!

Vocalizing

Was I a talker?

When would I vocalize?

What did it sound like? Describe it to me!

Did I sing? When would I sing?

Family Events and Occasions

Draw your own stick figure family here.

Birthdays

How did we celebrate my birthday?

Did I get presents? If so, what did I get? Were they wrapped?

Did I get to open them myself?

Did I have a cake or special treat?

Vacations

Did we go on vacations?

Was it road trips? Fly on a plane? A train? Stay-cations?

Did we ever go to a beach at an ocean or lake?

Was I a good swimmer? Did I like the water?

Did we go fishing? How about camping?

What other outside activities do you remember while we were on vacation or holiday?

Seasonal Holidays

Here are the story starters for Winter, Spring, Summer and Fall!

What holidays or events did we celebrate this season?

What traditions or rituals did we partake in?

Did I get presents? Did I give presents? What were they?

Did we eat special food? You know, the stuff I don't usually get to have the rest of the year?

Some Bunny woves Me!
Happy New Years Dawg!
HAPPY NEW YEAR
I have everything under control Rob. No worries!
I'm waiting for that darn rabbit!
This aint no drool pool party!
Hey! I'm A Pup-bee!
Winter has fluffy white stuff!

Winter Holidays

Spring Holidays

Summer Holidays

Fall Holidays

Other Special Occasions

(Weddings, Religious Events, Sports, Graduations, Family Picnics, etc.)

Did I Have My Own Babies?

Tell me about my children.

How many litters did I have?

What do you remember about my babies?

Did we keep any of them? Tell me the de-Tails!

How was I as a Mom? (or Dad)

Who was my "partner"?

If I didn't have babies…

What kind of a parent do you think I would have been and why?

Siblings; 2 and 4-Leggers

Did I have 2-legger brothers and/or sisters - you know, the ones without fur, feathers or fins? How many? What are their names?

How old were they when I came into their lives?

What did we do together?

Did I have any 4-legger brothers and/or sisters? How many?

What are their names?

Tell me more about them. Were they like me?

If I didn't have any siblings…

Did I have pals in the neighborhood who I hung with? Tell me about them, please!

Naughty Memories

What did I do?

Did I show any remorse?

Was I alone in this or did I have a partner in crime?

Rides in the Car!

Did I like riding in the car?

Did I get the shotgun seat? If not, where did I sit?

Did I have cool “shades” you know, sunglasses?

Did I “talk” to other dogs or people on the ride?

Was I in a seatbelt?

Where did I like going and where did I NOT like going?

Goin' to the Vet

Tell me about my overall health.

How was I about going to the vet?

Did I know when I was going? What gave it away?

Who was my vet?

What specific vet tails stick out in your memory?

Bath Time!

Tell me about getting baths…did I like them?

Was I a stinky smelly?

Who gave me baths?

Did I go to a groomer? Tell me about that.

Did you ever have to "de-skunkelize" me? Tell me the de-Tails!

My Favoritest Things About Me!

From my perspective,

how would I answer the following questions

and why? Give me the de-Tails please!

I was happiest when...

I was "really" a big grumpy grouchy pants when…

I got silly when...

I got sad or pouty when...

My favorite 2-legger food to snag was…

The worst thing I ever ate that I wasn't supposed to was...

My favorite season or time of year was...

I have to come clean; I was afraid of...

I'll deny it if you tell anyone, but my favorite 2-legger is…

I got you the most worriedest when I...

The bestest day of my whole life was when...

The Senior Years

The First Signs of Aging

How young was I when I started getting a "frosty" mug?

What physical changes did I go through?

Did I have any arthritis or any other age-related issues? What were they?

Was I on any medicine? If so, what were they? Was I good about taking them or did I fight you every step of the way?

What were the behavioral changes I went through as I aged?

Did I develop any illnesses? Tell me about it.

The Time

Making the Decision

When did you start thinking about my passing? What prompted that?

What were the signs?

Did I pass naturally, or did you have to make “the dreaded decision”?

What did the vet tell you about how you would know that it was my time?

Where did I pass? Who was there with me?

What other de-Tails do you remember about this time?

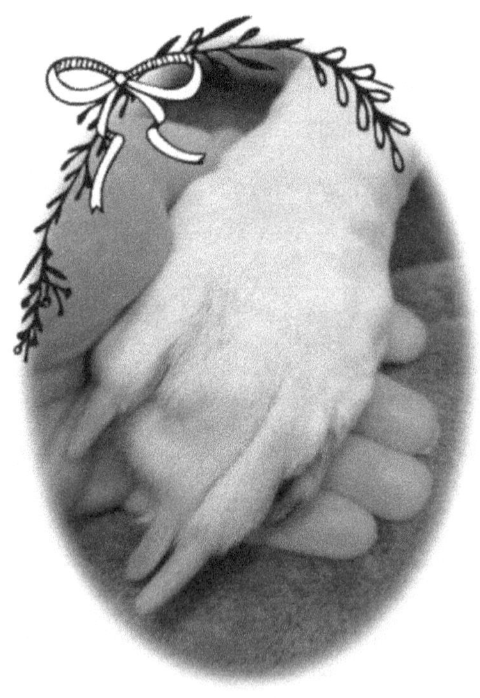

RUFF

A Pamism PawSpeak Acronym

Really

Un-**F**air

Feelings

The Love Letters

This is some of the most important work you will do on this journey. It is a time to focus completely on your loved one. It also may mean confronting your "woulda, shoulda and coulda's."

You will be writing two letters - the first is a letter from your pet to you, telling you how wonderful their life was with you and the rest of the family. If your pet is talkative and communicative, they will provide many examples chockfull of vivid de-Tails. Will this be difficult emotionally? Absolutely. But you will find it to be cathartic as well.

You will be using your imagination or, as I believe, your intuitive side, to do this work. Allow your beloved to whisper in your ear, and listen carefully, for it is in this space that you will find peace.

The second letter is from you to your pet. It's your personal tail, your turn to tell your pet exactly what they meant to you. And believe me, they want de-Tails! Imagine telling your loved one how you are feeling – your wishes and your regrets, all of it. If there are things you wanted to say at the time but didn't, here is your opportunity to say them. In this letter, it may be appropriate to apologize, ask for forgiveness, or express the feelings you may have never shared with another living soul (remember, our pets are the best secret-keepers, so you can trust them!). Don't be surprised at how forgiving and generous they are. Isn't that truly a part of unconditional love?

Once you have completed the two letters, that heavy burden of guilt – deserved or not - should begin to fade, liberating you and bringing you to a place of acceptance and forgiveness. Forgiveness does not mean condoning or excusing behavior; nor does it necessarily mean forgetting it. It simply means accepting that we may have done something we regret and are allowing ourselves a new perspective toward ourselves in relation to that action so that we can move forward.

Your Pet's Love Letter to You and Your Family

Write a love letter from your pet's perspective, addressed to you and your family, discussing the highlights of their life up to the day he/she passed.

What would your pet say to you and your loved ones?

What would your pet want you to know?

Please tell us all the de-Tails!

I've included a very special sample written by a very special friend, Pack member and client, Paula Almilli Ayala.

A Letter to Mama

I want to start from the beginning. The beginning is when you came to meet one of my siblings. I know you were there for a boy. There was only one boy and seven girls. Brother was my other half, and together, we made one puppy.

You saw that. We were not meant to be separated. You kept that promise to us and took us both to our new forever home.

You kept a picture of our fur-mom and fur-dad on the fridge for years. It's different with us doggies; we become family with those we share a home with. You are my Mama and that's okay. I've never been lonely or felt unloved. I always had Brother and you. Always. If you weren't home, I had Brother. There were only two times Brother and I were not together – when he had his surgery and when I had mine, but we always had you.

I always felt loved by you. Protected by you. You and I had broken hearts after Brother went to Heaven. Shattered hearts. We didn't know how to live without him. I was always the Big Sister and the one in charge of Brother, I worried constantly about how he was. Was he alone? Was he scared and looking for us?

You and I had a long time of silence and tears without him. You lived for me and I for you.

I have to confess that once I got sick and had to get my pancreas taken out, I chose not to work so hard at getting well again. I'm sorry I left you Mama. I had to go with Brother.

When you held my paw and talked to me the day my sick body passed away, I know you were there. I'm glad it was just the two of us at home together. I didn't know it then, but the heart attack I had in your arms was my way of giving my heart to you and to Brother. I saw you holding my body and crying and kissing me as I went toward the light.

In Heaven, Brother had made friends and he was there in the middle of the road waiting for me. We ran in circles around each other for so long! The first night with Brother again was the best sleep I've had in the sixteen months since I'd last been with him. We are complete again.

We love you constantly and still – and see you when you laugh and take funny pictures of new Brother, Jack-Jack. Know that we are happy and well and feel your love as if you are in the room with us, just as you did every day of our lives.

Thank you, Mama.

A Love Letter to Your Pet

And now it is your turn to write a love letter to your pet.

This is a letter of gratitude and appreciation. A time to profess your love.

Do you need to voice any regrets or ask for forgiveness?

What is it you never, ever, never want to forget?
Include all the de-Tails you remember.

I will Always
be your Angel!

I Am Your Angel

A Discussion About Spirituality and the Afterlife

Many of my clients and members of The Pack discuss messages and signs from the afterlife. Unconditional love is not just Earth-bound. I believe that our loved ones have the ability to send us messages to let us know they are still with us. They may be very subtle or grandiose in nature – it all depends upon their energy and personality!

I truly believe that our loved ones do not want us to suffer or be sad. Their wish is for us to be happy, healthy and productive.

Animals are nothing less than amazing. I believe they have a special brand of intuition that allows them to communicate with us on a completely different level, during their physical lives and beyond. Maybe it's a combination of senses they use to pick up on us, but they know - oh yes, they know.

Pet parents have a special mindset, as well; they are open to "possibilities." Some may call it imagination, but I like to think about this as more intuition or spiritual faith.

The discussion about the afterlife, heaven and the Rainbow Bridge can be a touchy subject. I believe all 2-leggers are free to decide for themselves what they want to take stock in. Personally, I do believe in the afterlife. I have had many experiences that have no other explanation. I am an intuitive. I have seen, smelled, heard and felt energy from those who have passed on.

The Bridge

In my writing I often refer to "The Bridge" – that special place where all animals go, a beautiful place where all animals I've loved go, where they can run freely without pain and in a youthful state. Reasonable minds can debate the existence of the Rainbow Bridge, but I choose to believe it does. It is my sincerest hope that I will one day be reunited with Roxy, and that each one of you will be greeted by your loved ones as well.

I call my perspective about the Bridge – the afterlife - "light." This holds no religious connotations; again, I leave this up to you to decide. I also like to look at the Bridge with a sense of fun and humor, because why not? On many occasions, I have told my Pack and clients that I have put in my application for a job at the Bridge (when it is "my time," of course), and that my GA (Guardian Angel) and best yella girl Roxy has already put in a good woof or two for her mama.

Bridge Belief Benefits

I think that having some level of hope or belief in the Bridge provides comfort and relief to grieving pet parents. Just as with our human loved ones who have passed, having faith that your animal friend is not only free from their Earthly pains, but the vision of youth and vitality makes it easier to bear their loss.

Messages and Signs from The Other Side

Now let's talk about contact with our loved ones who have passed on. This is something that many of The Pack and my clients want to know more about.

Messages and signs come in many forms; you can hear them, feel them, see them (physically or in your mind's eyes), smell them or even taste them. Most messages, however, come through our thoughts. Think of your mind like a radio receiver, picking up electrical waves. We can't see them, and sometimes they come through a frequency that is not so loud and clear, but nonetheless, they are there. In order to "catch" and recognize these messages, we must be receptive, open and aware.

Here are some examples to watch for.

- Hearing their presence
  - Collar tags jingling
  - Pawing. padding and claw scratching
  - Panting, breathing and snoring!
  - Music (i.e. a favorite song with special meaning pops into your head and/or comes on the radio or TV)
    - Have you ever been let's say, doing the laundry and a song "spontaneously" pops into your head? Sometimes it's a no-brainer – you "hear" what you would refer to as "our song," the one you would always sing while folding towels as your sweet pup sat right next to you. You *know* where this is coming from. Other times a bit more subtle (I believe our angels like to make it a little bit of a challenge). You may need to think more about the lyrics of a song and what they mean to you. Remember, we all have the innate ability to receive these messages, we need only open our minds and hearts to them.
- Thinking about your loved one
  - You spontaneously start thinking about your loved one - this is what I refer to as, a "telepathic text" message! It happens very often, so often perhaps that it is often overlooked. From my research, I have found that so many things "can" be a message. We may be missing something obvious from our loved ones.

- As a result, many pet parents feel disappointed that they aren't having visitation dreams, no cardinals perching on their hand. Stop putting pressure on yourself and give credit where credit is due. When getting telepathic texts, recognize that this is a message, one to give your full attention to.

- Dreaming about your loved one.
  - Have you ever had a dream about your pet, a dream that feels so real you wake up physically or emotionally drained? These are what's known as visitation dreams, and we discuss them often in The Pack. These dreams are ones you will never forget. In them, your pet may not communicate to you in a clear language or sequence – after all, that would be asking a lot! They are usually (but not always) brief, kind of bullet point communications that convey a message that they are doing well and not to worry. Remember, whether your loved one is a 2-legger or 4-legger, there is no "perfect" timeline for them to show up or a particular length of time in which they send their message. This is because linear time does not exist in the afterlife. The key here is to set aside your expectations and view your dreams with an open mind and heart.

🐾 <u>Feeling their presence</u>

- A cuddle in bed
  - A few Pack members discuss a familiar "climbing or jumping" sensation in their bed reminiscent of their pet's behavior. Others report a warm nuzzling up against the back of their legs,

like their cat used to do, or feeling whiskers or a tail against their skin.

- Sight - Seeing a presence
  - These are visual signs that come to you when you are awake. Remember, loved ones can use virtually *anything* to bring you a sign - a bird flying overhead, pennies on the sidewalk, a street sign, a song on the radio, a feather, repetitive numbers, something you see on the news, and so on. It can be subtle or grandiose, but anything visual can be a sign if it has meaning to you.
  - You may catch their image out of the corner of your eye, in your peripheral vision.
  - Waking from a dream and seeing your loved one near, then vanishing.
    - About a month after the passing of a very dear 2-legger friend, I woke up to find him standing over me and smiling. He looked as he did in his early twenties. Suddenly, the image shattered into a million pieces like broken glass and vanished. There was no doubt in my mind that he had come to say hello.
- Smelling their presence
  - You smell a familiar odor or aroma in an unlikely place that reminds you of your loved one.
    - Roxy's feet smelled like corn chips. I've lost count of how many times I would get a whiff of that odor after she passed. I knew immediately that it wasn't my imagination. I was smelling her "Frito feet," as we called them!
    - My father was a heavy smoker, after he passed of cancer, I would periodically get a strong whiff of

cigarette smoke. I got so accustomed to this happening that I would smile, say "Hello Dad," and go about my business.

- One client told me he smelled fast food cheeseburgers in his car, and knew it was his pup, because this was always a birthday treat to take a ride to the golden arches every birthday!

- Taste
    - This type of connection is usually reported in connection with 2-legger loved ones from the afterlife; for example, you may suddenly taste a favorite dish your mother used to make. That said, 4-leggers can do this as well, hopefully not with the taste of *their* food, but maybe a taste of their favorite 2-legger food as a treat! It has happened!
- Being guided and gifted
    - A very special type of message is sent through a new member of your family. I strongly believe and always say, "*When the right time is here, the right love will appear!*" Let's not forget that little chunk of yellow Lab fur at the base of Zuzu's chocolate Lab tail!

    - No matter what messages or signs you experience, I recommend keeping track of each one. Write them down in your journal and be sure to include as much de-Tail as you can remember, right down to the date and time. You never know whether collective messages have a deeper meaning!

I believe that our loved ones are thinking about us. As much as we may worry that we will forget important memories of our love, I believe they send us messages of the specific and special times of their lives so that we don't forget them. So, when you think you're not *fortunate* enough to find a white feather at your feet or the lights flickering in your bathroom, but you are thinking about your love, they are communicating with you more than you realize. Have faith that though your bond is never broken, it does change. Accepting this is part of the grieving process, and the sooner we do so, the easier the journey becomes.

What About You?

What have you experienced? Describe any messages, signs and "texts" below. Remember to record the date and time. Try to provide as much de-Tail as you can recall!

One Year from Today

Now that you have completed this part of the journey, I'd like you to take an intuitive look into the future – one year from now, to be exact. I want you to imagine a time when it might not hurt so much, when you are living on the other side of grief.

What does this next year look and feel like, emotionally, physically and spiritually? Start by bulleting out the first words that come to your mind, without censoring or editing. Allow the creative juices to flow.

Let these words germinate for a bit, whether for an hour or a day, and then return to expand in more de-Tail. When you are satisfied with the de-Tails, step back, take a look at what you have written. Highlight or underline key words that have risen to the top. Now, write them below.

These statements come from your heart. They are the start of your goals for the coming year. The next chapter in your tail is starting now.

____

____

____

____

____

____

Getting to the Other Side

I'd like to share some Tails from my Pack. I remember each one of their tails when coming into The Pack. I can't sugarcoat it, but I was pretty worried about each and every one of them at first, and then I witnessed transformation. I am sharing the following so that you too can visualize yourself coming out on the other side of your grief.

Tissue Alert!

Three and a half years ago I lost my Mr. Perfect. Oh, how I cried! I thought the tears would never stop. Then this lady appeared on my FB page and we talked. She listened as I went on and helped me so much with her understanding and kind, loving words. Though time has passed I still have his last toy, a little moose, under my pillow; I also can't seem to part with his blanket. If it hadn't been for this wonderful person and now great friend across the pond and the wonderful group we are all part of, I don't know how I would have

managed it. I have a new baby now, as nutty as a march hare and always under my legs, but a wonderful big brother to his seventeen-month-old 2-legger brother Alfie. I am forever grateful to that wonderful lady, my star sister, and the two other women who form our admin team.

– Edwena Martin

When my Kodi passed on to the Bridge, I was totally lost. The emptiness, the silence was deafening; the loss was so heavy I couldn't breathe much of the time. I could feel him near which was comforting but letting him go was best for both of us. That took some time. I jotted down some of his favorite things and memories because I was terrified I would forget. Even journaling was difficult, for I was afraid that in writing them down I would be letting those memories go. It was all so confusing. Then, after almost three years, I did a serious journal and was amazed at how I didn't forget anything. It was difficult but freeing. It's now been three and a half years, and I can honestly say I am NOT the same person. I will most likely always grieve for my best buddy, but I am sure I will see him again. I have accepted this loss as part of my journey. It's just my new normal.

– Brenda Giles

First and foremost, joining this wonderful page was a Godsend! To be in the company of people I've never met but who share my love of animals with no judgments - and having Pam here to hold my hand – has been priceless. When Bentley's cremains were returned to us, I put them in his treat tin. It's not fancy, but he loved those darn treats - I'd catch him staring at the tin with drool streaming from his mouth until I gave him one... It had to be his final resting place. I also had taken a couple clippings of his fur. Again, nothing fancy, just held together with masking tape and kept in a baggie. To date, I still take one of the pieces out and stroke my face, remembering spooning with him and burying my face in his back. His tin has a place of honor on a table with a portrait of him, all of the many collars he had, some of the last treats that I baked for him and a beautiful memorial poem picture given to me by a friend. It's his memorial! I cried a lot and many times, ran my fingers through his cremains...as crazy as that sounds. Each day I found it easier. I kept reminding myself how fortunate I was to have him for seventeen years. I also learned to forgive myself for making the "final decision," reminding myself that sending him to The Bridge was one of the kindest things I could have done, rather than watching him suffer. The pain is so real, but you will heal - truly! Just give yourself time. You will have a scar on your heart but choose to look at it as a reminder of a most wonderful life experience, to have been blessed with such an amazing creature. Finally, know that the best is yet to come, and that we will be reunited with our furry friends in the future.

-Kari Newcomer

Today I heard a song by Mickey Gilley called "Heartache Tomorrow" (you can find it on YouTube) and decided to dedicate it to my boy Rocky. I can't believe it's been over three years since I had to let him go. Honestly, it was pure hell those first few months. Time has helped but memories can be hard. I was told about this group and thought I would take a look. I am glad I did. Just the support alone I received from all members was amazing, and I am not sure where I would had been in my grieving process without it. Pam Baren Kaplan, our Pack leader, encouraged me to post, to share stories and pictures, as often as I needed, and I did. There were up days and down days, but far worse were the nights. I worked by myself at that time and my mind would not shut off. That's when I most often turned to Paws to post and comment. In the process I met a wonderful soul sister, Edwena Martin, across the pond. Since she was eight hours ahead we would talk for hours and still do. I think I would have been so lost without her. March of 2016 was a horrible month in many ways. Pam had some health issues, which was scary and hard on me. She was and still is my rock! I also connected with Cindy Collard, who always had the right thing to say and offered to make me a bear with Rocky's blanket. These three women, all of whom I have never met in person, have helped me beyond what my words can express. They have always been here for me. It takes time for the pain to go. It still comes and goes today. Anger is also still a major factor for me. Yet to all of you beginning this journey I will say that it does get easier. You might need to take it a day or an hour or a minute at a time. Don't hide your feelings, though, because this Pack will be there to support you even when your family or friends don't want to hear about how you

are sad or missing your furbaby. If you were to ask me right now how I am doing, I would tell you I am missing my Rocky and that there is a deep void in my life but overall I am strong and good. This is largely due to the love and support The Pack and our Alpha leader Pam have given me, and they will do the same for you.

-Ruth Eberlein Dow

To this day I remember the total despair and empty feeling I had when I had posted on a Labrador group that I belonged to about losing my best friend to cancer. I have lost loved ones before but this one cut deep; it cut to the bone. Shortly after posting, I received a private message from a very nice lady offering compassion and condolences; she also encouraged me to join a grief support group called Paws to Celebrate. I am so glad I did! I did not receive much support from my spouse, who thought Makena was "just a dog" and I should be able to get over it. I was made to feel like there was something wrong with me because I was grieving her. What I received at P2C was unconditional love, support and understanding. In the beginning, I posted often and let's just say I tend to be fairly verbose. I rambled, I cried; I ranted about my loss, my depression, and my feelings of despair. No one here judged me...they offered their ears, their shoulders to cry on and understood where I was at. They coached me and gave me words of encouragement. Most importantly I made new friends who truly "get" me. This has been a life-altering experience for me in many ways. The hurt of losing Makena is still there and always will be, but I have learned new coping mechanisms that help me to focus that grief in positive ways and to remember the good times I had during the ten years she was in my life. This kind soul gave me so much and made me a better person in the process. I owe much of my recovery to this group - the friends I have made here and of course the person that made it all happen - Pam Baren Kaplan. I owe you

a debt I can never repay. Thank you so much for everything. I hope I have helped others here as well. No one is alone in this group.

– Jay Canfield

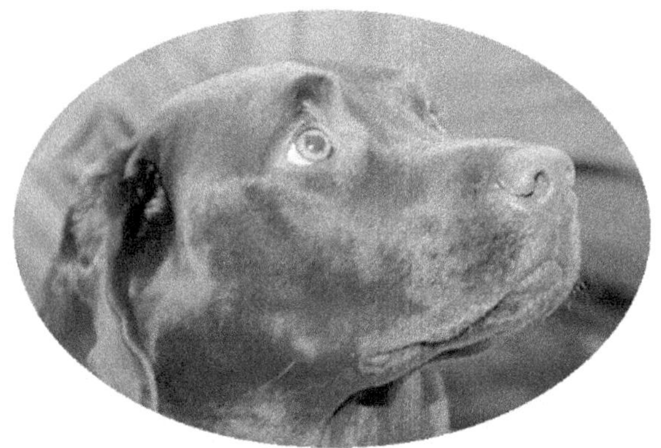

Section Three

Tools & Templates

FAQs to Get Started and How to Navigate if You Get Stuck

How and when do I begin? Is there a right time to do this work? A month after my loss? How about a year after?

You can begin this journey whenever it feels right to you! If you are wondering how you can allow recovery in, accept this as an affirmation that you are ready to honor the life of your lost loved one.

I'm apprehensive about doing this work because I've been "okay" lately. Will I get sadder and depressed all over again?

Yes, chances are you will experience the sadness again, but in a different way than before. This is because it is not a new loss, and because now you have a plan to get to the other side of grief.

Can I start this journal if they are still with me?

Absolutely. As the signs of aging become obvious, you may enjoy documenting many of the memories you shared. It can be an opportunity to get those big hugs and licks we all crave when they are physically no longer here with us.

What if I hit a wall while journaling certain sections? How do I get "unstuck"?

I will begin by answering this question with a question: are you spending too much time trying to get to the finish line? It may be a message to slow down and take a break. This can be emotionally draining. Set a time to do your work – i.e. an hour a day or three times a week - and adjust from there. This is a lifetime of love you are working on. Find your appropriate pace.

Getting to the love letter section, I'm hesitant to "go there." I am afraid I won't be able to do it!

I recommend that the love letters are done last, as all the work leading up to that point is geared to helping you come to terms with your loss and putting you in a mindset of gratitude. Yes, writing the letters will be hard, and yes, you will cry, but it will be a cathartic cry, a healing cry. Give yourself big kudos. It's tough work but the results are worth it!

My Tail Topics List

Depending on your unique relationship with your pet, there may be tails that don't apply to your story. If this is the case, make a list below of your own experiences and ideas, then take a blank copy of the template and journal them. Even if the tails do apply, this is a great opportunity to add additional memories.

1. ______________________________
2. ______________________________
3. ______________________________
4. ______________________________
5. ______________________________
6. ______________________________
7. ______________________________
8. ______________________________
9. ______________________________
10. ______________________________

Template Page for Tail Topics and Mind Map Memory

Insert Photo or Artwork

My Tail Topic/ Mind Map Memory Word/Idea: ____________________

My Memory, Our Tail…

____

____

____

____

____

____

Mind Map Template Instructions

1. Choose either an online mind map program, free hand or a grid.
2. Templates for grid and freehand are included on pages 210 and 211.
3. Write your pet's name on your map of choice.
4. Now write down all the words and ideas that come to your mind! (It's okay to come back to this page as many times as you need to.)
5. Add photos, keepsakes, or whatever you want to make this memory come to life!
6. For example and reminders, see pages 90-91.

Mind Map Grid

Pet's Name_______________________________________

For each word or idea, take a Mind Map Memory Page and share all the de-Tails! See the template on page 208.

Mind Map Free Hand

Write your pet's name in a circle; then free hand surround the name with all the words and ideas that come to mind. For each word or idea, take a Mind Map Memory Page and share all the de-Tails! See the template on page 208.

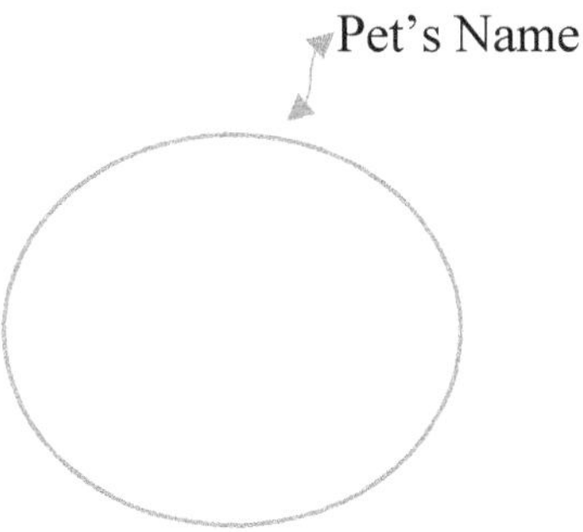

Making A Memory Garden

Healing Right Brain Activity

A "Memory Garden" is a special place where you collect your pets' special things (things you want to remember them by) and display them. Some of The Pack has referred to this place as their "Fur-ever Shelf." I love that! But no matter what you call it, it is a space for remembering, celebrating and honoring.

I'd like to share the following Tail from Jan Dicker, one of my lovely admins, about how she honored her love:

I am not sure that I am over the grief. It gets less over time, whether it be for two or four legged, but I'm never over it as such.

What we did after we lost Holly was look at all the photos we had taken over her eleven years. We then printed lots out, had them framed and placed them all over the house. We also had a special slate made with her photo and a nice saying, along with a jigsaw tree, which is the wood for October, the month she was born. This too we put her name on. These items, along with another framed photo and her ashes, are in our indoor remembrance area.

Outdoors, we have a section for our fur babies, with all their names and the dates of their birth and passing on individual slates.

The day we were going to pick up Holly's ashes, I went to a local garden centre and saw they had a full-size Labrador statue. That statue came home with us and now sits in the conservatory overlooking the garden; it has Holly's collar on.

Our special girl is never forgotten and is thought of every day.

The beauty of a Memory Garden is that it does not necessarily have to be outdoors, though of course it can definitely be made this way. We'll discuss both!

Usually this is the place where your urn or receptacle for ashes is placed as a focal point. Depending on your taste, you can go as minimalistic or as extravagant as you want. You can really create a very special place for one or all of your angels.

Here's a list of items The Pack and I came up with to get you started. Use it to make your Memory Garden your own!

1. Urn or receptacle for ashes
2. Paw Print
3. Photos
4. Toys
5. Tags
6. Motivational/Spiritual Quotes
7. Bowls (made into planters!)
8. Collar and Leash/Lead/Harness

What can you add to this list?

1. ______________________________
2. ______________________________
3. ______________________________
4. ______________________________
5. ______________________________

If you decide to build outdoors, some additional weather resistant items may include:

1. Garden monuments and statuary
2. Plant a tree (Many of The Pack have said they buried the ashes with the tree, so they become a part of nature. How beautiful is that!)
3. Flags
4. Seasonal flowers. I love forget-me-nots, a perennial that comes up each spring. Perennials are great because they remind us to celebrate the cycles of life and rejuvenation.
5. A bench so you can sit and be with your thoughts.

What can you add to your outdoors list?

1. ____
2. ____
3. ____
4. ____
5. ____

I encourage you to share your own Memory Garden. Send me a photo and tell me the tail at pam@pawstocelebrate.life. We just may add this to our online gallery!

"Remember, you are never alone. We are walking just slightly ahead of you, periodically looking back to make sure you're okay."

In Closing

Roxy and I thank you for taking this journey with us. Remember, though you have finished the book, your own journey is just beginning.

For more, I invite you to visit my website (included on the Resources page) where you can schedule a private grief session with me and/or register your angel/s for the AWA and Happy Heavenly Birthday Announcements. You can also sign up for my newsletter, which will keep you current on my events, classes and upcoming books. I've got a children's book series starring Roxy in the works!

With all our love!

Arf!

Pam and Roxy

About Pam

Pam Baren Kaplan is a writer, jewelry designer and Certified Professional Coach specializing in pet loss grief recovery and life and corporate coaching. In August 2015, she founded Paws to Celebrate, a highly interactive, supportive and healing global community that supports grieving pet parents as they work through the loss of their 4-legger friends.

Previously, Pam spent over three decades in corporate employee development and management; human resources, operations and project management. An emergency triple bypass changed the course of her life, leading Pam to devote herself completely to her purpose and passion for helping people and animals. Today, in addition to coaching clients around the world, she continues to serve as Leader of The Pack of Paws to Celebrate. She also designs handmade jewelry using the ashes of her clients' beloved pets-in-spirit.

Pam lives in a suburb of Chicago with her husband Lou and their two 4-legger girls; Zuzu and Frankie. She also has two wonderful 2-legger children, Jon, Dani, a daughter-in-law Adrianne, and a grandoggie, Penny.

About Paws to Celebrate Pack

Before I formally introduce you to The Pack, I feel it's important for you to understand how this community of 2-legger kindred souls got started. I must also thank my daughter Dani for suggesting I start this group. With her usual wisdom and insight, Dani knew what I needed most was to find my own tribe, and that in helping them through their grief, I would find and heal myself.

In the Beginning

I started Paws to Celebrate on August 14, 2015. Having already cultivated a fairly large Facebook "friend-base," I invited my family and friends with pets to join. Some had already experienced pet loss and were eager to be a part of a like-minded community.

In the beginning, growth was slow. Back then Facebook didn't promote its groups like they do today, so I had to rely on member word of mouth *evangelism* -. in other words, I begged family members to invite *their* family and friends to join. I also tried joining other Facebook groups and "gently" promoting Paws, but that didn't work too well. Group administrators (myself and my Pack included) can be a bit territorial, and I found myself bounced from more than one group. Each time, it was back to the drawing board. Then an idea came to me. I fondly refer to this procedure as *trolling.*

I began within the pet groups I already belonged to, mostly Lab groups because my girls, Zuzu and Frankie, qualified me as a Lab parent. As I participated in and connected with these communities, I began to see many posts from members whose Labs had passed. Along with these posts I noticed a pattern: an incredible outpouring of condolences, followed by the griever fading into the everyday chatter about new puppies and how one gets their Lab to stop chewing on the living room furniture. I also noticed that the grieving pet parent stopped posting about their pain. It seemed they had been forgotten.

I didn't forget, though. I would find myself wondering, "What happened to that person? How is he or she doing? How are they managing their grief?" I saw this as my opportunity to help.

Treading carefully so as not to step on any toes, I sent a private message to the admins of a few groups to see if they would allow me to approach grieving pet parents. For the most part, I was permitted to make a one-time invite to the grieving member. At first it felt so uncomfortable, but it worked! I got a few members to join! I was also getting thumbs up, actual LIKES and a few hearts on my posts from sympathizing members. Some even asked to join Paws so they could offer support to grieving pet parents!

This wasn't a foolproof procedure, however. I was slapped on the wrist by a few groups who felt that while my purpose was noble, they do not allow posting of other groups in their group. Okay, okay I get it! I wouldn't want someone pirating my members either.

In the meantime, Paws membership was continuing to increase. The slow start turned out to be a blessing, for it gave me the opportunity to create the kind of grief support group I envisioned. This meant recognizing that each member's grief - and the length of time they need to go through the grieving process - is as unique as the bond between them and their pet. Hence our mission statement: "To listen, to love and support, for as long or as short as you need."

I also wanted Paws to Celebrate to be more interactive and

engaged than other groups I had seen. Being a pet loss grief recovery professional and life coach, I very much wanted to provide a safe space where grievers could just "be" with their grief or chose to speak freely about their pain in a non-judgmental environment while getting a strong sense of community ("The Pack"). I also wanted to provide current news on pet loss to help bridge the lack of information our culture provides. Finally, I decided to be on the light side of spiritualism so that The Pack would feel free to discuss their individual beliefs.

We are not the largest pet loss support group, but I do believe we offer a unique environment for grieving pet parents because we are focused on healing as well as compassionate comforting. Yes, other groups want you to get to the other side of grief, but at Paws, we show you *how*. We encourage participation and engagement. Sharing stories, or tails, helps expedite the healing process. I also like to bring some fun and a sense of humor to lift the spirit. To this end, we hold regular Pack Events, such as:

Ask The Pack and Tell Me a Tail. Members participate in a Pack poll, or survey on a topic that pet parents can relate to. This is important for a few different reasons. First, regular engagement gives members a good reason to return to the group often. Second, talking about these times is very cathartic; and third, it helps keep their memories strong and alive. Such events also have a viral effect, meaning that in telling one's stories, members provide support to others while they work through their own grief.

Another Paws event is AWA, or Angel Wing Announcement. Members "register" their angel by going online at my website www.pawstocelebrate.life to submit the information about their angel in order to be announced. We then honor that date as a part of whole-life celebration. This weekly event has been in existence almost as long as Paws itself.

We also have themed days; for example, "Tattoo Tuesday" is a

Pack favorite. Here, members get to show the ink they got (or plan to get) to honor their angel. It has been a successful repeat event over the years. It also provides other members with interesting ways to give tribute to their pets.

These events have facilitated so many friendships across the globe. Members get to know and appreciate each other, and they are comforted by the fact that I am here to help whenever they need extra support. They have also learned that I can be one silly 2-legger at times. I'm sure I have made a few eyes roll with some of my corn ball sayings (Pawspeak) both on Facebook and throughout this book. If it has made you smile, I've done my job.

My ultimate goal has and always will be to rebrand pet loss grief. Finally, our rituals, traditions and education are coming out of the dark ages so that pet parents can get the support and assistance they need. People are beginning to understand that, just as with 2-legger grief, grieving a furry, finned or feather friend is not a sprint but a marathon of complex emotions one must work through. Though we may be tempted to give up and give into the pain, we persevere. Why? Because we know that is the last act of love we can give our pets in this lifetime, so we'd better make it a "good grief." No, we will make this the best grief!

I couldn't do any of this without the support of The Pack, which I have come to love as members of my own family. Many of these 2-leggers came to this group in deep despair over their own loss, only to transform before my eyes, largely through the love and support they gave and received from their fellow members. To my admins, I give a special thanks: Jay Canfield, Cindy Collard, Jan Dicker, Ruth Dow (Tails to Celebrate, Paws little sister) and Edwena Martin. You are the best Pack within a Pack and I love you all!

Like many groups on Facebook today, Paw's is a closed group, meaning one must ask to join. We ask three questions to prescreen members to be sure they are joining for the *right reason*, not to use this grieving support group to market their products. In this way, we can protect The Pack and the integrity of our mission. For more information, see the Resource page for getting “Packed.” I promise, if you join you will be welcomed with open paws!

Bibliography

Burgess, Lana. Eight Benefits of Crying and Why it's Good to Shed a Few Tears. www.medicalnewstoday.com. 2017

Capra, Frank. Director. It's A Wonderful Life. Liberty Films. 1947

Coppala, Francis Ford. Director. The Godfather. Paramount Pictures . 1972

Coren, Stanley Phd, DSc,FRSC. Do Dogs Grieve Over the Loss Of Companion Animals. www.psychologytoday.com 2016

Fireman, David LCSW. Suggestions for Grief Journaling. www.griefcounselor.org. 2018

Greenfield, Sherry. The Rising Popularity of Pet Cremations in the Tri- State Area. www.heraldmailmedia.com. 2016

James, John W. and Friedman, Russell. The Grief Recovery Handbook New York, NY. Harper Collins. 2009

Kubler Ross, Elizabeth and Kessler, David. On Grief and Grieving New York, NY Scribner Publishing. 2005

Orloff, Judith MD. The Health Benefits of Tears www.psychologytoday.com. 2010

Ramis, Harold. Director. Groundhog Day. Columbia Pictures 1993

Spector, Nicole. Can Smiling Trick Your Brain Into Happiness www.nbcnews.com. 2017

Stang, Heather Grief Journaling Tips and Prompts www.mindfullnessandgrief.com. 2013

Resources

Getting Packed: Paws to Celebrate, "The Pack" Facebook Group

www.facebook.com/groups/pawstocelebrate

Paws to Celebrate Website:

www.pawstocelebrate.life

Pam Baren Kaplan's email:

pam@pawstocelebrate.life

Thunder Labradors:

www.wisconsinlabradors.com

Free Gift - Download the Journal Pages:

https://www.pawstocelebrate.life/workbook

A Very Special Acknowledgement Page

This book is a labor of unconditional love and I would like to thank the following 2 and 4-leggers who have contributed their photo memories and words to this book.

Adrianne Hanley & Penny Marshall

Angela Smith & Cicada

Brenda Giles & Kodi Bear

Cindy Collard & Maggie Mae

Edwena Martin & Harry, aka Mr. Perfect

Virginia (Gini) Moncur & Annie

Hilary Maye Ramsey & Seamus

Jackie Arnold & Cha Cha

Janet Ann Dicker & Holly & Nessa

Jay Canfield & Makena

Jen Barksdale & Luna & Tyson

Jessica Bobadilla & Cookie & Pennie

Kari Newcomer & Bentley

Katherine Jung & Gigi aka Gigi Angel, Gigi Ballerina

Kris Wacker & Magus, Copper, Jinx, Odie & Zeus

Linda & Lexi Puppy aka Mouth or Boo Boo

Lisa A. Frost & Sebastian aka Bash

Lindsay F. & Shelby

Lisa Smith & Wonder

Lisa Lechner & Chloe

Lisa M. Slattery & Oreo

Pam Baren Kaplan's Roxy, Zuzu & Frankie

Patty Marrali & Rosie aka Ro Ro

Paula Almilli Ayala & Baby Girl, Jack-Jack, Monster & Socrates

Rob Yates & Sam

Ruth Dow & Rocky & Samson

Sandi Ikovitz & Arlo

Susan Gronewold & Buddy

Susan Dubow & Itchy

Terry Traynor & Teagan

Tracy Cromey & Chloe & Kasey

Theresa Winkelmann & Brandy

Vicki Stocking & Moose

And I would also like to shout a BIG ARF and Thank You to:

Rick Reeves & Jerry Attere, Head Shot Photographers. Thank you both for taking these beautiful photos of one of my favorite places in the universe, my back yard where so many of my memories of Roxy originated.

Kris D. Carr, my goddess of all Illustrations for this book! This was a crazy-fun journey, so glad you went "willingly" along with me!

Shanda Trofe, or, as I lovingly refer to her as my "Fairy Godmother." You have been instrumental in helping me birth this baby. Without you guiding me, encouraging me to get out of my own way to get the creativity and passion flow, I'd still be scribbling in a spiral notebook only daydreaming of becoming an author! Thank you so much for making this real.

Printed in the USA
CPSIA information can be obtained
at www.ICGtesting.com
CBHW061503131024
15790CB00014B/1104